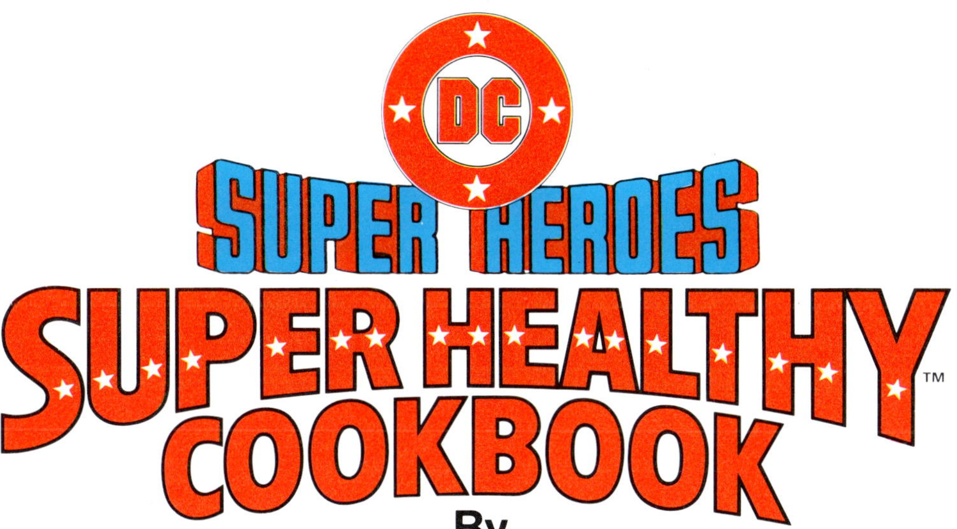

By
Mark Saltzman
Judy Garlan
&
Michele
Grodner

WARNER BOOKS

A Warner Communications Company

Warner Books, Inc., 75 Rockefeller Plaza,
New York, N.Y. 10019

 A Warner Communications Company

First printing: May 1981

10 9 8 7 6 5 4 3 2 1

Printed in the United States of America

**Library of Congress Cataloging in Publication Data**

Saltzman, Mark.
DC Super Heroes Super Healthy Cookbook.

SUMMARY: Gives directions, accompanied by explanatory line drawings, for a variety of kitchen-tested recipes from simple snacks to a Mother's Day breakfast tray.

1. Cookery—Juvenile literature. [1. Cookery]
I. Garlan, Judy, joint author. II. Grodner, Michele, joint author. III. Title.
TX652.5.S24 641.5'123 80-22749
ISBN 0-446-51227-3

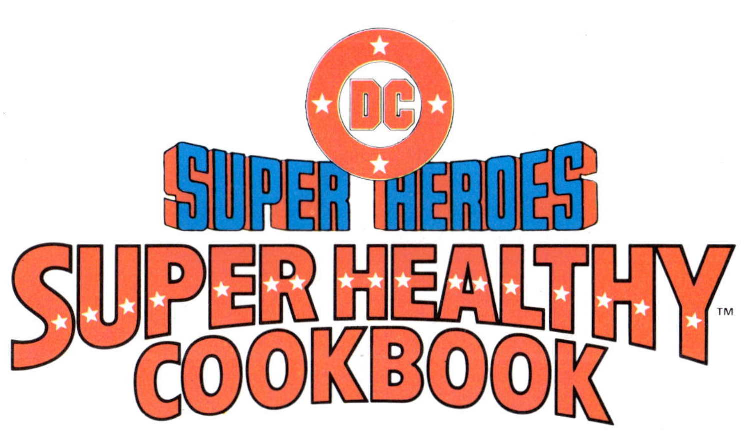
DC
SUPER HEROES
SUPER HEALTHY™
COOKBOOK

Editor: **JOE ORLANDO**

Photography: **STEVE EISENBERG**
Art: **ROSS ANDRU, LEO DURANONA and DICK GIORDANO**
Lettering: **GASPAR SALADINO**
Based on an idea by **JENETTE KAHN**

And special thanks to:
Laurie Sutton, Todd Klein, Shelley Eiber, and Tony Tollin

Cover Credits:
Design by Judy Garlan
Photography by Steve Eisenberg, Jack Adler

Written by MARK SALTZMAN
Designed by JUDY GARLAN
Recipes by MICHELE GRODNER
Foreword by DR. JOAN GUSSOW

# FOREWORD

By Joan Dye Gussow, Ed. D.

Well, this does it! It's now clear that my generation was sold a bill of goods. They convinced us that good nutrition was dull, that eating healthy food meant giving up whatever tasted good, and that cooking was sexist, life-denying drudgery—to be avoided at all costs. Now DC Comics comes along with a cookbook like this one and shows it all up as a pack of lies.

Maybe where we went wrong was with boiled vegetables—all those overboiled vegetables our mothers made us eat. (Commissioner Gordon would *never* have picked vegetables for a secret mission when I was growing up—frankfurters, maybe—but not vegetables). Or maybe it was all those clever women we saw on television—the ones who served their families scrumptious looking meals out of their grocers' freezer cabinets.

Oh, certainly I had a cookbook. It had little pictures of teaspoons and measuring cups and it told you how to make fudge brownies and white cake with jam frosting. If you were a kid, cooking meant dessert. After all, who wanted to boil vegetables?

Nobody boils vegetables in *this* cookbook. Vegetables get turned into salads, and robots (!); they get oven fried and speed stirred; and generally there's a lot of fooling around designed to make them quickly delicious. But there are no instructions like there were under "vegetables" in the cookbooks of my youth: "boil 30 minutes or until tender."

Now, of course, we had to eat those veggies anyway—mushy and tasteless as they were—because no one had much money during the Depression and you had to fill your plate up with something. Meat was expensive. But when we all got richer, we knew what had to go—those boiled vegetables. And when the meat had pushed all the green beans and spinach off the plate and we all began to get fatter (because that steak wasn't all protein) we decided we'd better give up the bread and potatoes, too . . .

And around that time we started to see those women on TV. They seemed so happy, so pleased with themselves—and their families seemed so delighted with their freezer food. And we realized that if it was good to get food on the table fast, it might be even better to skip the kitchen altogether and let the colonel and Ronald and the king and the cowboy do the cooking for us.

So here we are in the 1980's, eating too many calories, too much fat (so *that's* what came with the protein!) and too much sugar and too much salt. We worry about our weight, we talk about eating "junk," we promise ourselves to do better. And all the while real honest-to-goodness food is out there waiting for us—including those veggies, low calorie, low fat, low sugar, low sodium . . . and *crunchy! Now* they tell us that even potatoes aren't fattening.

But don't get the idea that this book is just about vegetables. It's about food, about main dishes and party dishes and snacks, and breakfasts—and even desserts (but no white cake with jam frosting). And while it isn't exactly accidental that the food this book is about is healthy and delicious, that's not the only reason to give *Super Heroes Super Healthy Cookbook* houseroom. What's wonderful about this book, from the standpoint of someone who became a nutritionist *despite* boiled vegetables, is that it gives the lie to the whole set of myths that led my generation astray. Healthy food is often tastier than unhealthy food, men too can cook, good nutrition isn't dull, and—above all, *cooking can be a pleasure*. If you don't believe it, just turn the page.

## ABOUT DR. GUSSOW

Dr. Joan Gussow is presently the Chairperson of the Department of Nutritional Education and an associate professor at Teacher's College, Columbia University. In addition to her teaching duties, Dr. Gussow has served as a nutrition consultant for various firms, and written numerous articles on the subject of health. Her most recent book, THE FEEDING WEB: ISSUES IN NUTRITIONAL ECOLOGY, was published in 1978.

# CONTENTS

AND SPEAKING OF ***CONTENTS,*** REMEMBER TO CHECK THE INGREDIENTS OF ANY PACKAGE YOU BUY. THE FIRST ONE LISTED IS THE ONE THERE'S THE MOST OF. SO MAKE SURE YOU'RE NOT BUYING MOSTLY WATER OR SUGAR. LOOK CLOSELY AT THE LABEL.
GRAPE JELLY
INGREDIENTS
CITRATE

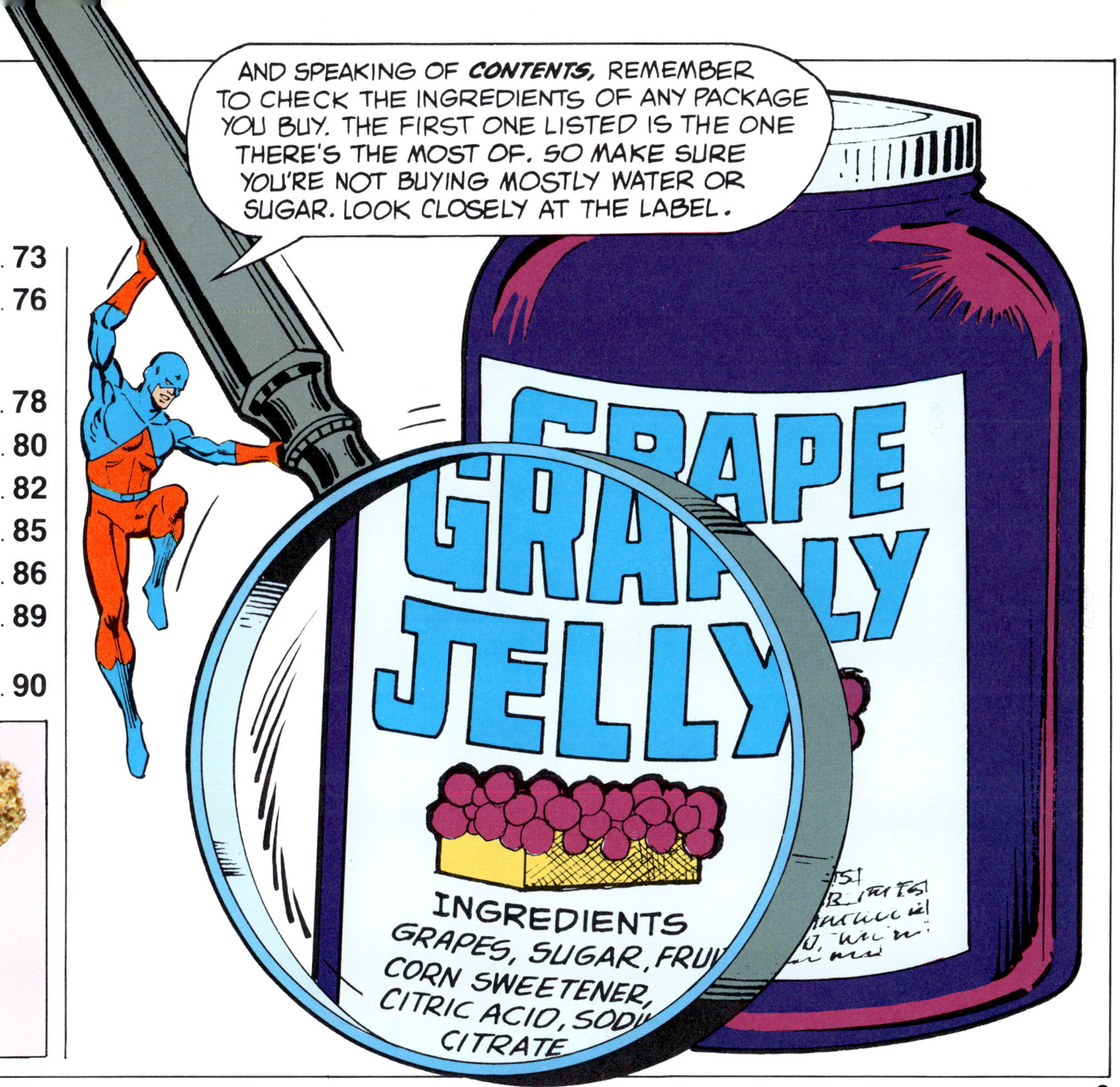

# INTRODUCTION

By Michele Grodner, M.S.

Eating "right" in the past meant eating three well-balanced meals full of vegetables a kid hated, while his mother stood over him making sure each bit of food was well-chewed and swallowed.

But times have changed. You now have the chance to make many more food decisions than ever before. Most kids eat lunches at school and choose what they want. In many homes, both parents work, so kids come home and pick out their own snacks.

Eating well should not be a struggle between parents and kids. You should take on the responsibility of caring for your bodies as soon as possible. How you eat affects how you're able to roller skate, or throw a ball, or learn in school. By eating well, you not only feel better today, but you're laying a good foundation for how you will feel as an adult.

Food keeps you alive. You need food for growth, energy, and feeling good. But it's what's in the food that keeps the body working well.

You need to eat protein foods because protein helps the body do repair work, fights infection, and keeps the body running smoothly. Protein-powered foods like meats, fish, chicken, cheese, milk, and eggs can also give you energy.

In our food supply there are two kinds of carbohydrates: refined and unrefined. Unrefined carbohydrate foods are in their whole form, like whole wheat flour. Refined foods have been processed, either cooked or separated, and that changes the form of the foods. Processing the food can often cause the food to lose some of its food value. For example, a baked potato is an unrefined form of carbohydrate full of food value. But potato chips, which are refined potatoes, have been deep fried and lose a lot of food value from being cooked that way.

Good sources of unrefined carbo hydrates are whole grains and breads, potatoes, wheat bran and dried fruits

Vitamins are also in foods. Not only do they keep the skin and eyes well, but they are also needed to keep the body growing and working well every day. Vitamins are in many foods, especially fruits and vegetables.

You need food to keep your body

running smoothly, and you also get energy from food. Energy is measured in calories, just as space is measured in feet and inches. A calorie is the measure of the energy that's in a food. Some foods are high in calories but have little else that is good. Such foods are called "empty" foods, or sometimes, junk foods. Sugar, candy, cakes, potato chips are examples of junk foods. They don't help the body grow, although they may give some energy for a short time. The best bets, for the body, are those foods that not only have calories, but have good nutrients, also.

You can become overweight or "fat" by taking in more calories or energy than you need. The extra calories or energy are stored as fat on the body.

Naturally if you eat too little food for your body's energy needs, you will become thin.

There is a balance between the energy taken into the body and the energy the body uses.

In most cases, you can have control over your body by eating the right kinds and amounts of foods.

## FOOD TIPS

- Boost your protein intake by adding wheat germ. Sprinkle it on sandwiches, add it to a banana smoothie, or eat it as a cereal.

- Add sprouts to sandwiches instead of lettuce. Try vitamin-packed alfalfa, mung, or lentil sprouts.

- Soda is a bad buy. It provides empty calories, a lot of sugar, and leaves you thirsty for more. Buy a fruit juice instead.

- Vegetables are a prime source of vitamins, especially when eaten raw. When vegetables are cooked they lose some vitamins. The best way to cook vegetables is to steam them and eat them crisp.

- All three forms of sweeteners, white sugar, brown sugar, and honey, have one thing in common. They make foods sweet, but provide little else.

What's wrong with sugar anyway? Sugar greatly increases the chances of

getting cavities. No amount of candy bars are worth sitting in a dentist chair with the drill running. Also, sugar adds unneeded calories to food so that if you do eat lots of sweets you may end up overweight.

The problem with our food supply today is that sugar often sneaks up where it doesn't belong. We end up eating a lot more sugar than we mean to. If we knew that sugar was only in desserts we'd be able to control how much sugar we eat. But foods prepared by food companies, often have sugar added. Reading the labels of foods can tell you whether sugar is added or not. Look for words like: dextrose, corn syrup, sugar, honey, corn sweetener, molasses, and brown sugar.

- When you buy peanut butter, check the label and buy the brands that have the fewest additives. Peanut butter doesn't need any form of sugar to taste good. It really doesn't even need oils or salt.

- Use carob instead of cocoa or chocolate. When cocoa is made into chocolate, fat and sugar are added. The problem with chocolate is that along with the cocoa you also get all that fat and sugar. Carob is made from ground up seed pods of a special evergreen tree, and contains more vitamins and minerals than cocoa, and is lower in fat. Plus, it is not as bitter as cocoa so less sugar is needed to make a sweet tooth happy.

- Choose whole wheat flour and bread over white. All wheat flour is made from the wheat berry. White flour is made just from the part of the wheat berry called the endosperm. The rest of the wheat berry, the wheat germ and the bran, are taken away. And the wheat germ and bran contain vitamins, minerals and protein not found in the endosperm.

Whole wheat flour consists of the whole wheat berry—with all the nutrients in it.

## SAFETY TIPS

- Be extra careful when using the oven or stove. Make sure you don't burn your hands—use thick, dry potholders to touch the pots.

- If you have a gas stove, make sure the pilot light is on. If you're not sure what this means, check with your Mother or Father.

- When slicing or chopping vegetables, use a cutting board, so you don't damage the table or counter top.

- When peeling or paring vegetables, make sure the knife moves away from you. Otherwise, it could slip and cause a cut.

- To avoid electrical shock, make sure

your hands are dry before plugging in any appliances.

- When you unplug an appliance, pull it out by the plug, not by the cord attached to the plug.
- Wash knives separately from other tools, and be careful of the blades.
- Make sure the stove and oven are turned off when you're done with them.
- If grease should catch fire, do not pour water over the flame. Call for someone's help right away. The fire should be put out with a $CO_2$ chemical extinguisher. If the fire is in a pan, put the cover on the pan to smother the flames, or pour baking soda on the fire.

## COOKING TIPS

- Read the recipe first. Make sure you have the right ingredients, and you know what to do.
- Get the O.K. from an adult before you start working in the kitchen.
- Wash hands well with soap and water before beginning.
- Get out everything you need for the recipe.
- Measure foods carefully. Use measuring spoons and cups, not regular spoons and cups, for measuring.
- Know the names of the tools you'll be using. They are listed inside the front and back covers of this book.
- Have a place for every tool you're using. Put it back there when you're finished with it. If it needs to be washed after you use it, let it soak in soapy water until you're ready to wash the dishes.
- Make sure the kitchen is clean when you leave it.

### ABOUT MICHELE GRODNER

Michele Grodner has most recently worked as a consultant in nutrition education for UNESCO and *Sesame Street*. Michele is currently devoting her energies to lecturing at Montclair College, pursuing her doctoral degree at Teacher's College, Columbia University.

# COOKING TERMS

There are a few cooking terms you'll need to know before you start working with the recipes in this book. This list will give you the meanings of some of the terms. Look them over, and turn back to this list if you forget what any of them mean.

To mix ingredients with a spoon. If you're mixing over heat, use a wooden spoon or a metal spoon with a plastic handle so it doesn't get hot while stirring.

## MELT

Making something solid turn into a liquid by heating it over a low flame. To *thaw* means to let something frozen stand at room temperature until it un-freezes.

There are three kinds of flame: low, medium and high. On a gas oven, look at the flame to see how big it is. On an electric range, just set the dial.

To put in the freezer compartment of your refrigerator until frozen. Make sure the food is in something freezer-proof, like a plastic bowl or ice cube tray.

## SIMMER

To cook slowly over a low flame. Simmering is different from boiling, which uses a high flame and gets a lot of action going in the pot. Simmering just makes small bubbles.

To take the skin off a fruit or vegetable. The best tools to use are a peeler or a paring knife, to do the peeling. (Unless, of course, you're peeling a banana.)

Mixing food together. This may be done with a big spoon and a bowl, or in a blender, depending on what the recipe says. When using a blender, be sure to check what speed the recipe says to use.

## SLICE

To use a sharp knife to cut strips or circles no more than about ¼ inch thick. Slicing should be done very carefully on a hard surface, like a cutting board.

To break an egg into a bowl or a cup. You're supposed to try to do it without getting the insides on the table or the pieces of eggshell in the bowl.

To quickly stir ingredients. An egg beater or electric mixer is sometimes used. For beating eggs, you can just use a fork and stir real fast.

To cook food in a hot oven. Check the temperature the recipe calls for, and set the oven at that number. Be sure there's an adult around before you turn on the oven.

Fruits and vegetables need to be washed before cooking. Just hold them under running water and rub. Hands also need washing before they handle food.

To chop food into very tiny pieces. The only way to do this right is with a grater. Rub the food along the holes of the grater, but watch out for your knuckles.

To coat a cold pan with a small amount of oil, margarine or butter. Use a napkin or a paper towel to spread the grease evenly around the surface of the pan.

To cook in a greased frying pan. Make sure the pan is the right size for what you're cooking, and the grease is hot, but not smoking, before you add food.

When using a knife to cut food into small pieces, work on a cutting board, not a table or counter top. And be sure that your fingers stay far from the knife's blade.

To bring a liquid to the point where it rapidly bubbles. Usually, boiling is just for water. When you're cooking food in a pot, you usually *simmer* it.

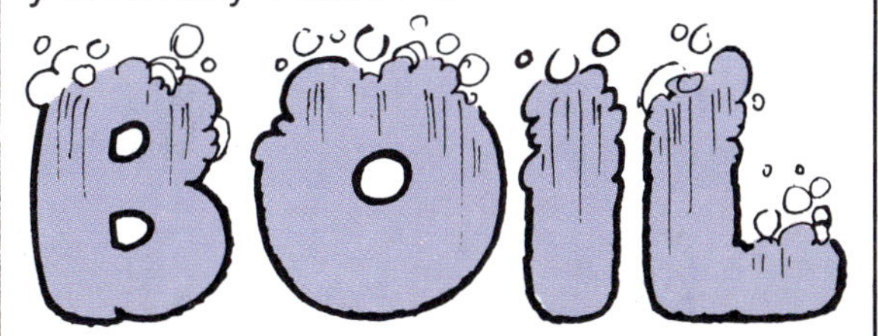

# BREAKFAST

Just as a car needs fuel to run, your body also needs fuel to get going. The fuel is food. When you wake up in the morning, with dinner many hours behind you, your tank is empty. Your body will run on empty, but not very long and not very well. The best way to refuel is to eat early in the day, and make yourself a good breakfast.

You can eat food for breakfast that's different from the usual bacon, eggs and cereal. Do you only eat peanut butter sandwiches at lunchtime? Try one for breakfast. What about leftovers? Instead of waiting till later in the day, have a chicken leg or some tunafish for breakfast protein.

What, you don't eat breakfast? Try to get in the habit slowly. A quick breakfast drink might be good to start with, like the Banana Smoothie or Pineapple Sip. Or try a slice of wholegrain bread with peanut butter, ricotta or cheddar cheese. Add a glass of milk or juice and in no time, you have prepared and eaten breakfast.

Included in this section are a variety of breakfast meals. Some are real quick to make—they're good for school days. The ones that take longer are better on Saturday and Sunday mornings when you have time to spend in the kitchen.

CRACK

# BAT-BANANA SPLIT BREAKFAST

**FOOD YOU NEED:**
(serves 1)

½ Cup Cottage Cheese
1 Banana
1 Tablespoon Wheat Germ
1 Tablespoon Raisins
1 Tablespoon Nuts
1 Tablespoon Coconut
2 Teaspoons Yogurt
2 Strawberries or Blueberries

**TOOLS YOU NEED:**

Ice Cream Scoop or Large Spoon
Knife
Banana Split Dish or Shallow Bowl
Measuring Spoons

1. WITH ICE CREAM SCOOP, MAKE TWO BALLS OF COTTAGE CHEESE. PUT THEM IN DISH.

AND NOT ONLY ARE BANANAS FULL OF VITAMINS, BATMAN, BUT THEY ALSO HAVE A-PEEL!
2. PEEL BANANA AND SLICE IT LENGTHWISE. PUT ONE HALF ON EACH SIDE OF DISH.
3. SPRINKLE WHEAT GERM AND COCONUT ON ONE BALL. PUT RAISINS AND NUTS ON THE OTHER ONE.
4. PUT ONE TSP. YOGURT ON EACH BALL.
5. TOP EACH BALL WITH A FRESH STRAWBERRY OR BLUEBERRY.

# MA KENT'S WHOLE WHEAT PANCAKES

SOMETHING SMELLS TERRIFIC! BY USING MY X-RAY VISION I CAN SEE THAT MA KENT IS MAKING THOSE SPECIAL PANCAKES OF HERS. I'D LOVE TO KNOW HOW SHE GETS THEM TO TASTE THAT GOOD, BUT SHE KEEPS THE RECIPE IN A LEAD BOX!

**FOOD YOU NEED:**
(serves 4)

- 1½ Cups Whole Wheat Flour
- 4 Teaspoons Baking Powder
- ½ Teaspoon Salt
- 1 Tablespoon Brown Sugar or Honey
- 2 Eggs
- 2 Cups Skim or Whole Milk
- 3 Tablespoons Vegetable Oil
- 1 Teaspoon Vegetable Oil

**TOOLS YOU NEED:**

- Measuring Cup
- Measuring Spoons
- Large Bowl
- Mixing Spoon
- Ladle
- Frying Pan or Griddle
- Spatula
- Paper Towel or Napkin

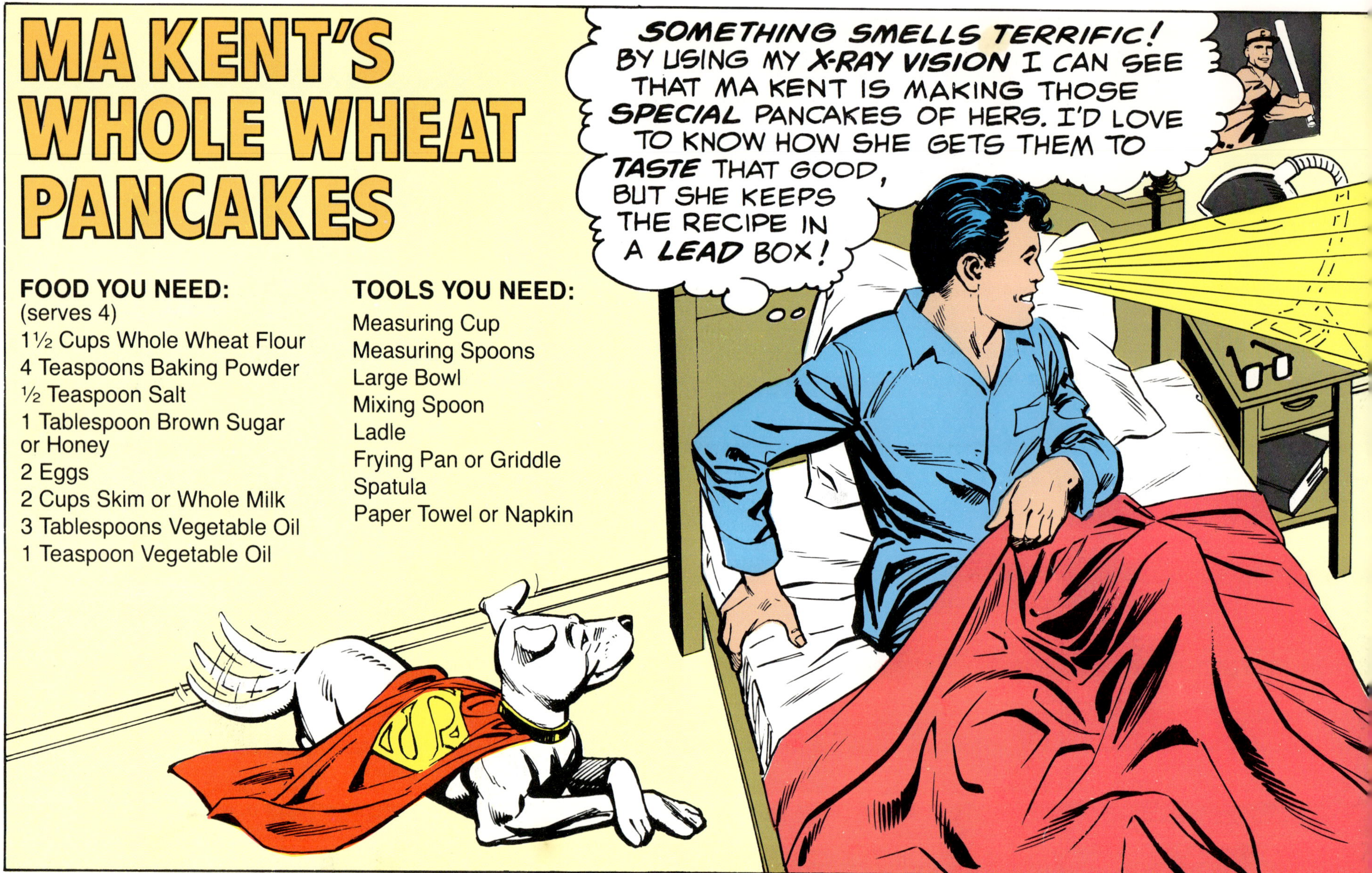

1. PUT FLOUR, BAKING POWDER, SALT, SUGAR AND EGGS INTO A LARGE BOWL.
2. ADD MILK AND 3 TABLE-SPOONS VEGETABLE OIL.
3. STIR WITH MIXING SPOON UNTIL BATTER IS SMOOTH.

4. BEFORE PUTTING PAN ON STOVE, GREASE THE PAN BY SPREADING ONE TEASPOON OIL WITH PAPER TOWEL.

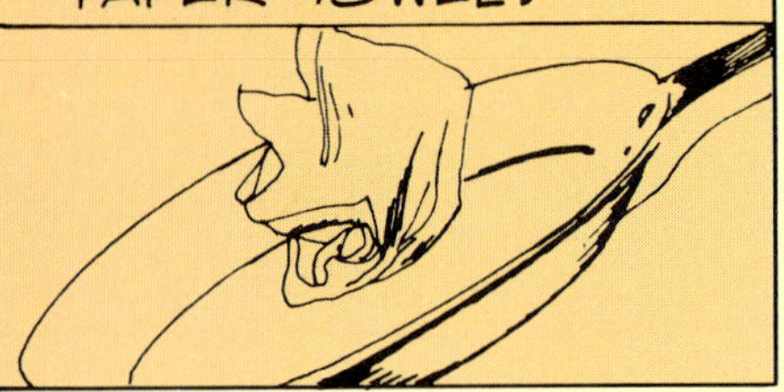

5. PUT PAN ON STOVE AND HEAT ON MEDIUM FLAME UNTIL VERY HOT, MAYBE ONE OR TWO MINUTES.

7. WHEN THE PANCAKES PUFF UP AND HAVE TINY BUBBLES, FLIP THEM OVER WITH A SPATULA.

8. ABOUT ONE MINUTE LATER, WHEN PANCAKES GET BROWN ON BOTH SIDES, REMOVE THEM FROM PAN. REPEAT UNTIL ALL THE BATTER IS USED...

## SUPER SUGGESTION

Why stop with a plain, dead-pan pancake? Here are some ways to decorate your breakfast plate:

### THE PERSONALIZED PANCAKE

Pour pancake on griddle, and flip.

Pour the initials you want onto the cooked side, then flip again.

Cook for about a minute, then serve.

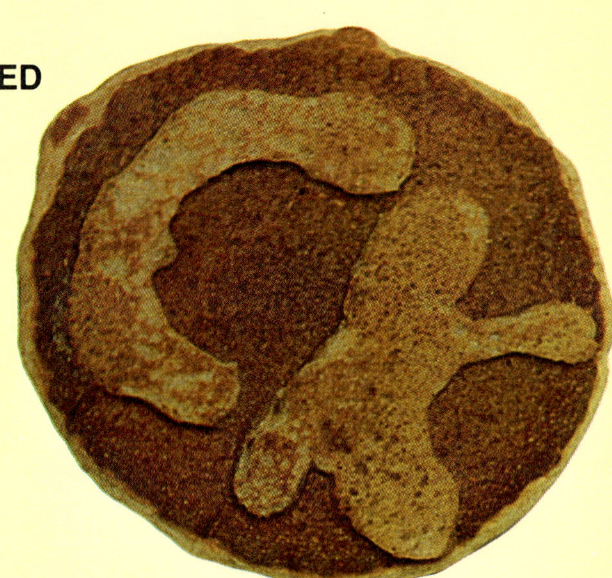

## THE PANCAKE SPEAKS

Pour pancake onto griddle but leave a little extra trail behind it.

Cook like a regular pancake.

When the cooked pancake is on your plate, add a message written in syrup, jam or apple butter.

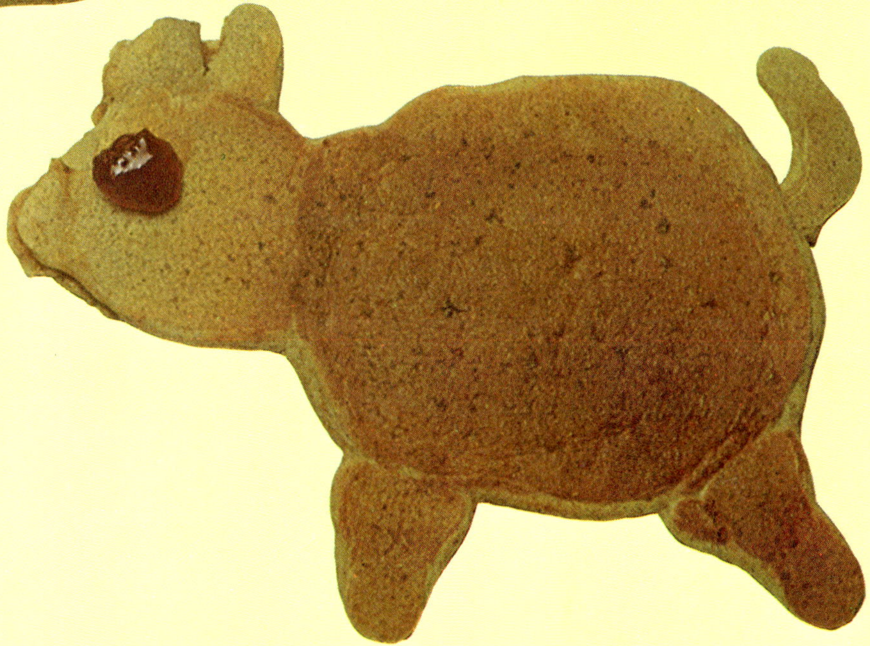

## LITTLE GRIDDLE CREATURES

Pancakes can be made in any shape. Try making the pancake version of animal crackers. Make any animal you want, and use apple butter or jam to add details.

MA KENT'S PANCAKE HINTS

200°

TO KEEP PANCAKES WARM UNTIL YOU FINISH COOKING THE WHOLE BATCH:

1. SET OVEN TO 200°. PUT THE PANCAKES ON A PLATE AND LEAVE THEM IN THE OVEN.

**OR**

2. COVER THE PANCAKES WITH A CLEAN NAPKIN OR DISH TOWEL.

SERVE WITH TOPPINGS SUCH AS PEANUT BUTTER, BUTTER, SYRUP, YOGURT, CUT UP FRUIT, WHEAT GERM, SESAME SEEDS AND APPLESAUCE.

YOU'LL NOTICE, HAWKGIRL, THAT THESE EGG-BIRDS ARE MERELY SCRAMBLED EGGS AND TOAST WITH A BEAK OF CHEESE STUCK ON. YOU'LL FIND THAT THE ***EGG-BIRD*** BREAKFAST WILL GET YOUR DAY OFF TO A ***FRYING*** START. *Heh-heh.*
I JUST HOPE YOU CAN CRACK EGGS BETTER THAN YOU CRACK JOKES, HAWKIE.

# HAWKMAN'S EGG BIRDS

**FOOD YOU NEED:**
(serves 1)
2 Eggs
2 Tablespoons Skim or Whole Milk
1 Tablespoon Wheat Germ
1 Tablespoon Butter
or Vegetable oil
Pinch of Salt
1 Slice Whole Wheat Toast
Piece of Cheese
2 Raisins

**TOOLS YOU NEED:**
Small Bowl
Measuring Spoons
Fork
Wooden Spoon
Small Frying Pan

4. MELT BUTTER IN FRYING PAN. HEAT UNTIL BUTTER IS BUBBLY, ABOUT ONE MINUTE.

5. POUR EGGS INTO PAN. STIR WITH WOODEN SPOON, SCRAPING BOTTOM OF PAN. STIR UNTIL EGGS ARE FIRM.

6. PUT COOKED EGGS ON PLATE. MOLD THEM INTO SHAPE WITH SPOON.

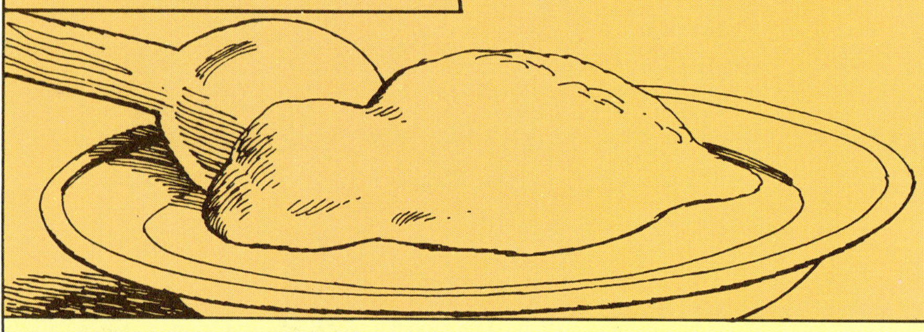

7. CUT TOAST IN HALF DIAGONALLY TO MAKE WINGS. ADD CHEESE FOR BEAK AND RAISINS FOR EYES. USE TOOTHPICK TO HOLD BREAD-WINGS TOGETHER.

## HOW TO CRACK AN EGG

- Gently hold the egg in your hand. DON'T squeeze it.
- Lightly tap the middle of the egg on the edge of a bowl.
- Tap the egg a little harder until you make a small crack in the egg.
- After you've made that first crack, hold the egg with two hands, one on each end of the egg. Your thumbs should be near the crack.
- Now tap the egg a little bit harder, so the crack gets bigger. When it does, QUICKLY hold the egg over the bowl and pull the two halves of the egg apart. Let the insides just drop into the bowl.
- The whole trick is pulling apart the eggshell after you've made the crack. Do that last step carefully and you won't have to worry about shells in the bowl or yolk on the floor.

# KRYPTON KRUNCH CEREAL

**FOOD YOU NEED:**
(serves 12—⅓ cup each)

2 Cups Toasted Wheat Germ
1 Cup Bran
½ Cup Sunflower Seeds
½ Cup Toasted Sesame Seeds (see note on other side of page)
¼ Cup Coconut

**TOOLS YOU NEED:**

Measuring Cup
Large Bowl
Mixing Spoon
Large Jar

YOU CAN MAKE THIS KRYPTON KRUNCH CONTAINER BY JUST CUTTING OUT THE LABEL ON THE NEXT PAGE AND STICKING IT ON A PLAIN JAR. AND DON'T WORRY ABOUT CUTTING UP THE COOKBOOK. CUT CAREFULLY, AND THE RECIPE WILL STAY IN THE BOOK.

YUMMIER THAN A BOX OF JUNK CEREAL

MORE NUTRITIOUS THAN A VITAMIN-ENRICHED SNACK

ABLE TO FILL YOU UP IN A SINGLE SERVING

IT'S A CEREAL! IT'S A GRANOLA! IT'S --

UNFROSTED

UNPUFFED

# KRYPTON KRUNCH

UNSMACKED

UNPOPPED

DOES NOT CHANGE COLOR, TURN INTO CANDY OR COOKIES OR MAKE FUNNY NOISES...

...JUST LIES QUIETLY IN THE BOWL AND LETS YOU EAT IT!

Ingredients: Wheat germ, bran, sunflower seeds, sesame seeds, coconut and NO JUNK.

**A)** TO PUT LABEL ON JAR, FIRST CUT ALONG BLACK DOTTED LINE, THEN ALONG RED DOTTED LINE.

**B)** SPREAD THIN COAT OF PASTE OR GLUE ON BACK OF LABEL.

**C)** STICK LABEL ONTO LARGE JAR.

**1.** PUT ALL INGREDIENTS IN LARGE BOWL. MIX.

**2.** PUT CEREAL INTO LARGE JAR AND STORE IN REFRIGERATOR.

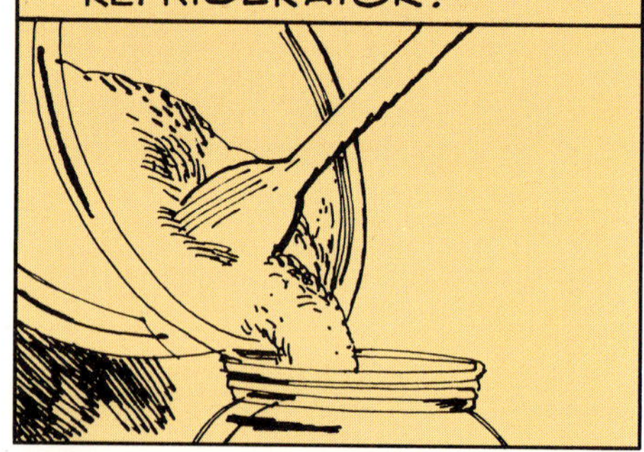

NOTE: TO TOAST SESAME SEEDS, PUT SEEDS IN A HEAVY FRYING PAN. FRY OVER A SMALL FLAME; STIR SEEDS WITH A WOODEN SPOON UNTIL THEY'RE GOLDEN IN COLOR. STORE SEEDS YOU DON'T USE IN A GLASS JAR.

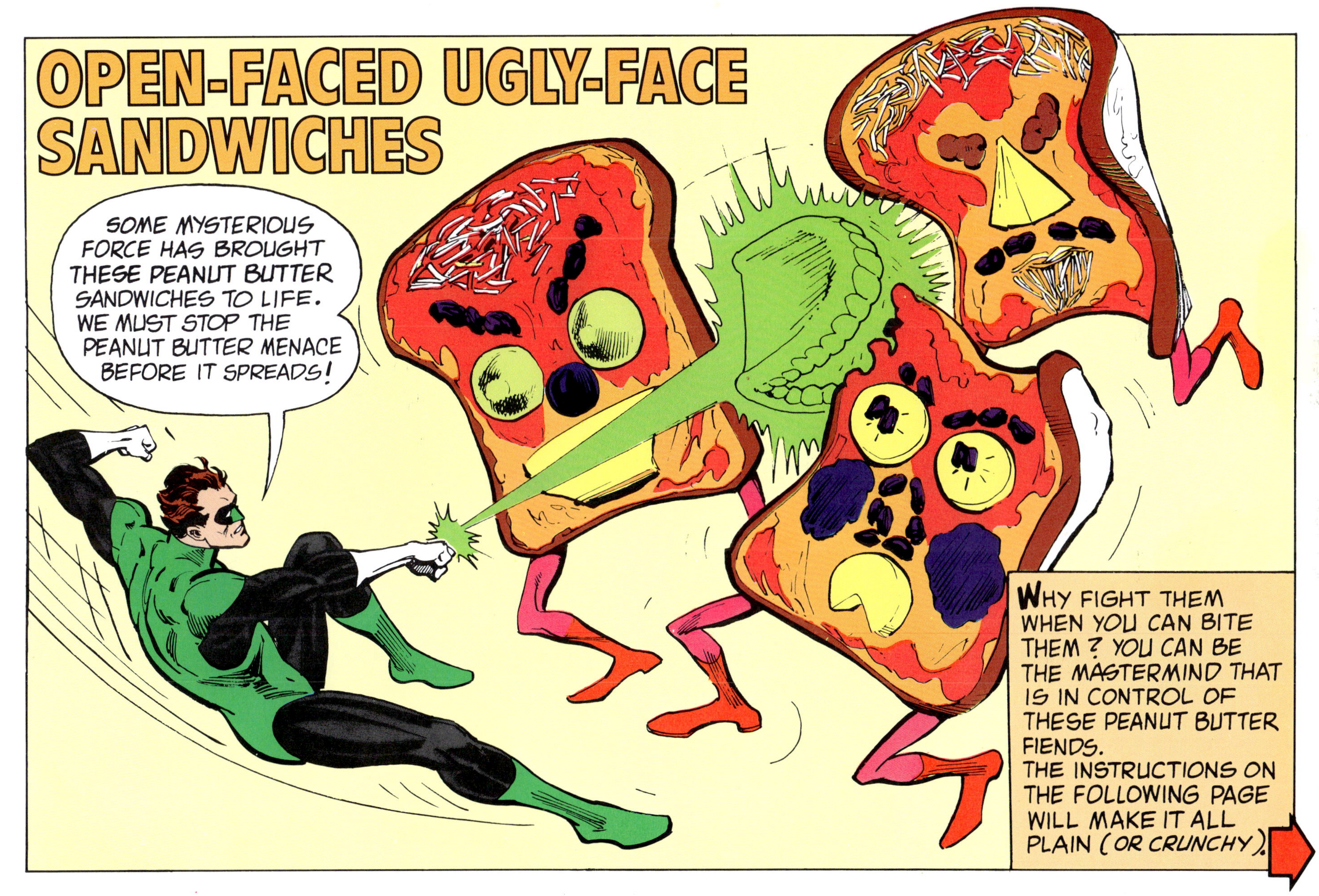
OPEN-FACED UGLY-FACE SANDWICHES
SOME MYSTERIOUS FORCE HAS BROUGHT THESE PEANUT BUTTER SANDWICHES TO LIFE. WE MUST STOP THE PEANUT BUTTER MENACE BEFORE IT SPREADS!
WHY FIGHT THEM WHEN YOU CAN BITE THEM? YOU CAN BE THE MASTERMIND THAT IS IN CONTROL OF THESE PEANUT BUTTER FIENDS.
THE INSTRUCTIONS ON THE FOLLOWING PAGE WILL MAKE IT ALL PLAIN (OR CRUNCHY).

1. SPREAD PEANUT BUTTER ON BREAD.

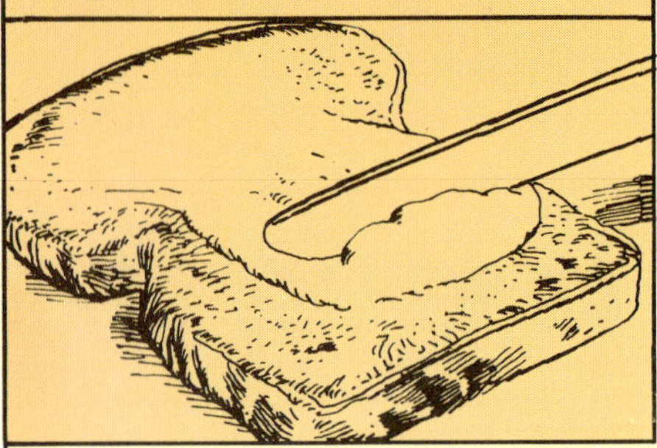

2. IF YOU WISH, YOU CAN COVER WITH APPLE BUTTER OR APPLESAUCE.

3. USE BANANAS, RAISINS, NUTS, COCONUT, OR WHATEVER, TO MAKE FACES.

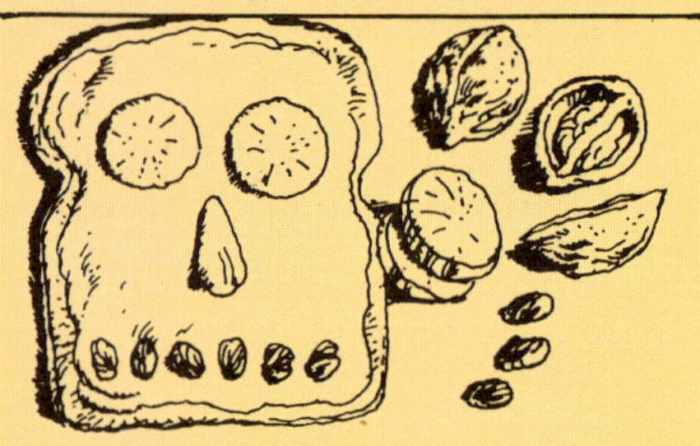

**FOOD YOU NEED:**
(serves 1)

1-2 Tablespoons Peanut Butter

1 Slice Whole Grain Bread

Plus any of these—
Apple Butter, Applesauce, Bananas, Raisins, Nuts, Coconut

**TOOLS YOU NEED:**

Bread Knife

Spoon (for Applesauce, or Apple Butter)

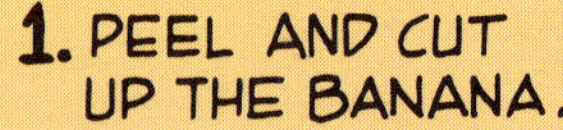

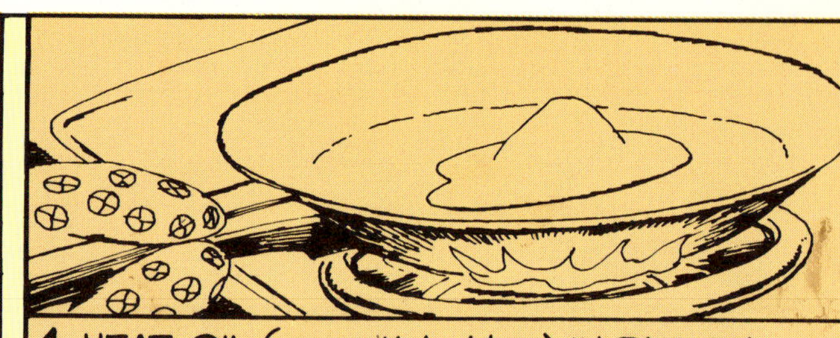


# THE INVISIBLE BANANA FRENCH TOAST

**FOOD YOU NEED:**
(serves 2)
1 Egg
½ Banana
½ Teaspoon Cinnamon
3 Slices Whole Grain Bread
2 Teaspoons Butter or Vegetable Oil
Serve with Maple Syrup, Applesauce or Yogurt

**TOOLS YOU NEED:**
Small Knife
Measuring Spoons
Blender
Soup Bowl
Fork
Frying Pan

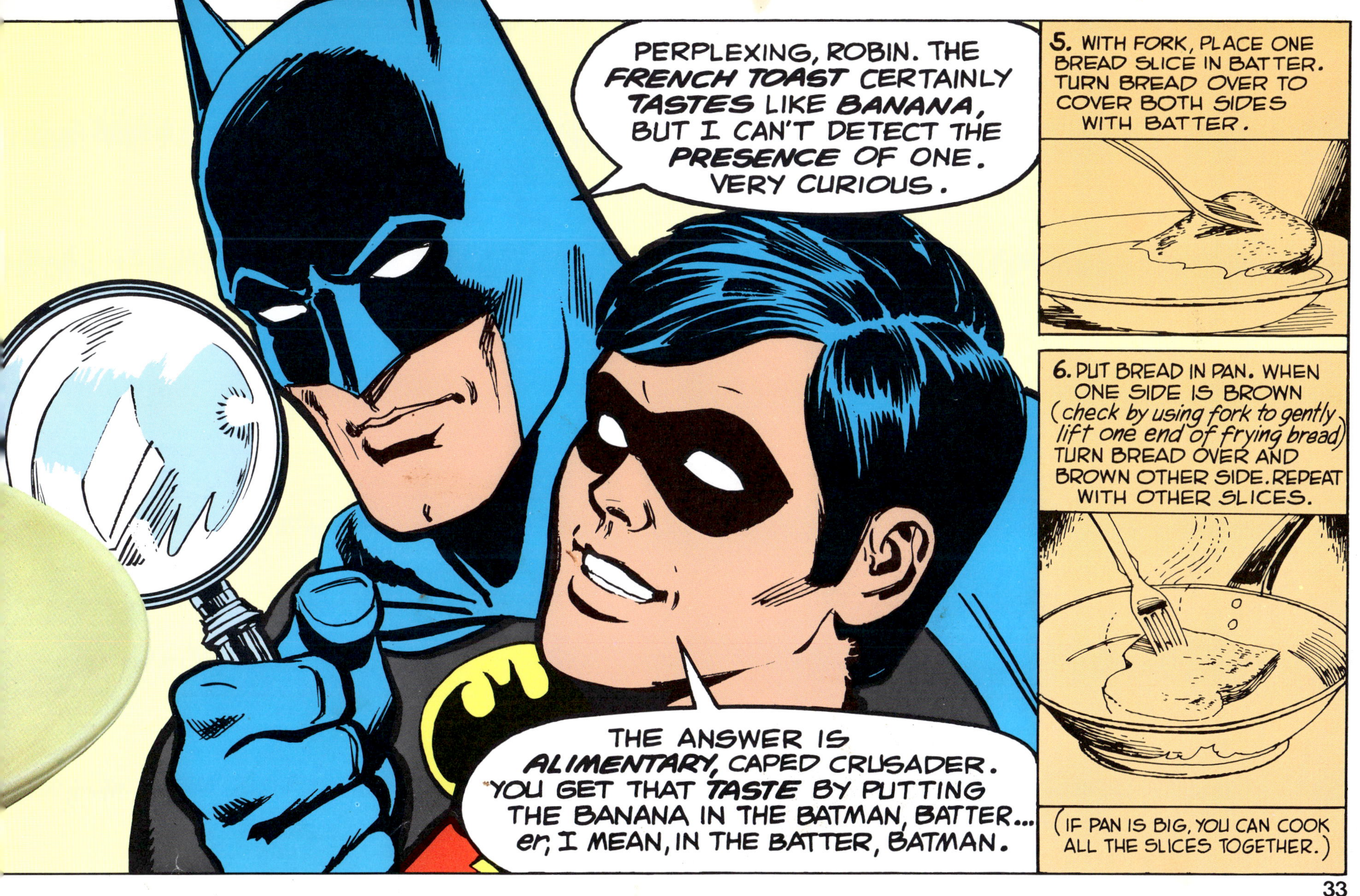
PERPLEXING, ROBIN. THE FRENCH TOAST CERTAINLY TASTES LIKE BANANA, BUT I CAN'T DETECT THE PRESENCE OF ONE. VERY CURIOUS.
5. WITH FORK, PLACE ONE BREAD SLICE IN BATTER. TURN BREAD OVER TO COVER BOTH SIDES WITH BATTER.
6. PUT BREAD IN PAN. WHEN ONE SIDE IS BROWN (check by using fork to gently lift one end of frying bread) TURN BREAD OVER AND BROWN OTHER SIDE. REPEAT WITH OTHER SLICES.
THE ANSWER IS ALIMENTARY, CAPED CRUSADER. YOU GET THAT TASTE BY PUTTING THE BANANA IN THE BATMAN, BATTER... er, I MEAN, IN THE BATTER, BATMAN.
(IF PAN IS BIG, YOU CAN COOK ALL THE SLICES TOGETHER.)

# BREAKFAST DRINKS IN A FLASH

## BANANA SMOOTHIE

**FOOD YOU NEED:**

1 Cup Skim or Whole Milk
2 Tablespoons Yogurt
1 Egg
1 Banana (broken up in pieces)
1 Teaspoon Honey (if you want)

**TOOLS YOU NEED:**

Measuring Cup
Measuring Spoons
Blender

# PINEAPPLE SIP

**FOOD YOU NEED:**

1 Cup Pineapple Juice
1 Egg
1 Teaspoon Honey
(if you want)

**TOOLS YOU NEED:**

Measuring Cup
Measuring Spoons
Blender

# SNACKS

Wherever we look, something is tempting us to snack. TV commercials, billboards and friends all try to get us munching.

But there are two problems with snacking. If you snack on the wrong kinds of food, like candy and other high-calorie junk foods, you might not be hungry for a meal. The junk food would take the place of real food and you'd get less nutrients for the same calories.

The other problem with snacking is that even if you do eat full meals, the snacking will put too many calories in your body. If you eat more calories than you can use, your body stores them as fat. Many people who are overweight got into a bad snacking habit when they were young.

But snacking can be O.K., depending on the snack and the time of day. You might want an afternoon snack to divide the "schoolday" from the "playday." Just be sure you snack on nutritious foods, like fresh fruit, raisins, cheese, raw vegetables and fruit juice. A snack should just be a light munch, not a second lunch or an early dinner.

There are some snacks in this section for those days when an apple just isn't enough. Try these recipes, and then experiment on your own.

pop
pop
pop

# CRACK-A-JOKE POPCORN

**FOOD YOU NEED:**
2 Tablespoons Vegetable Oil
⅓ Cup Popping Corn
½ Cup Butter
1 Teaspoon Molasses
⅓ Cup Honey
½ Cup Peanuts

**TOOLS YOU NEED:**
Large 2 to 3 Quart Saucepan
Small Saucepan
2 Large Cakepans
Large Bowl

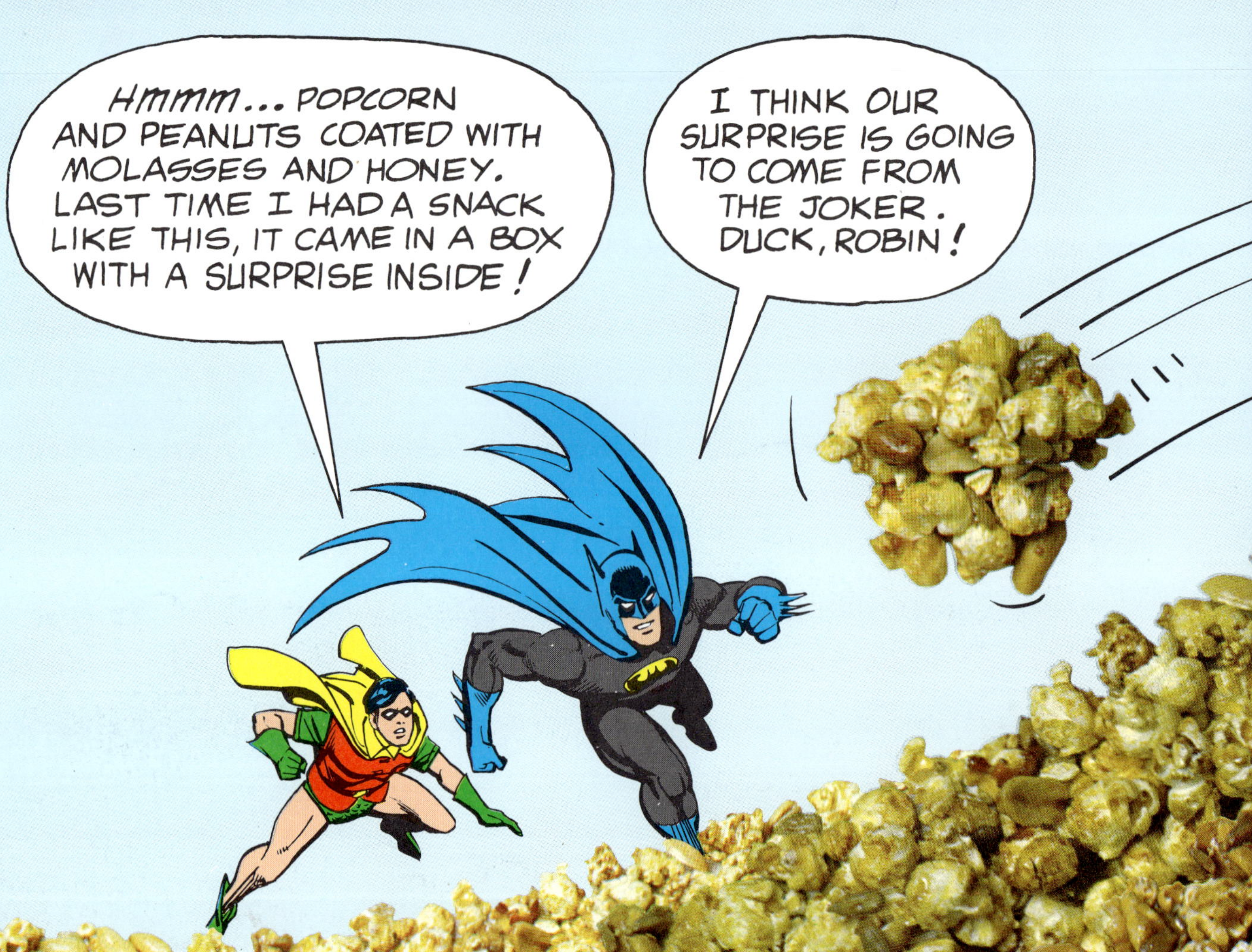

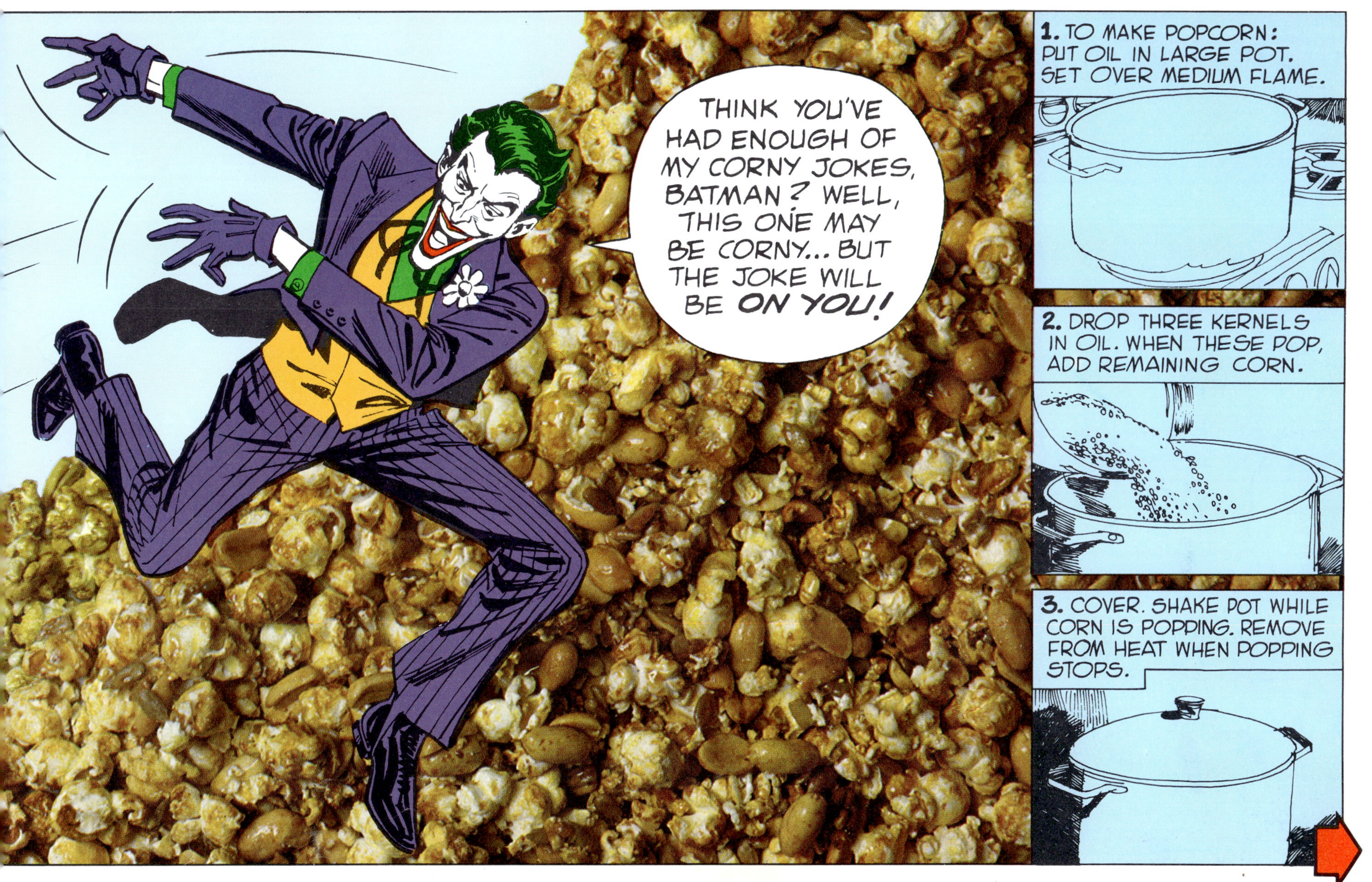
THINK YOU'VE HAD ENOUGH OF MY CORNY JOKES, BATMAN? WELL, THIS ONE MAY BE CORNY... BUT THE JOKE WILL BE ON YOU!
1. TO MAKE POPCORN: PUT OIL IN LARGE POT. SET OVER MEDIUM FLAME.
2. DROP THREE KERNELS IN OIL. WHEN THESE POP, ADD REMAINING CORN.
3. COVER. SHAKE POT WHILE CORN IS POPPING. REMOVE FROM HEAT WHEN POPPING STOPS.

4. LET POPCORN COOL, AND MELT BUTTER IN OTHER POT.

5. ADD MOLASSES AND HONEY.

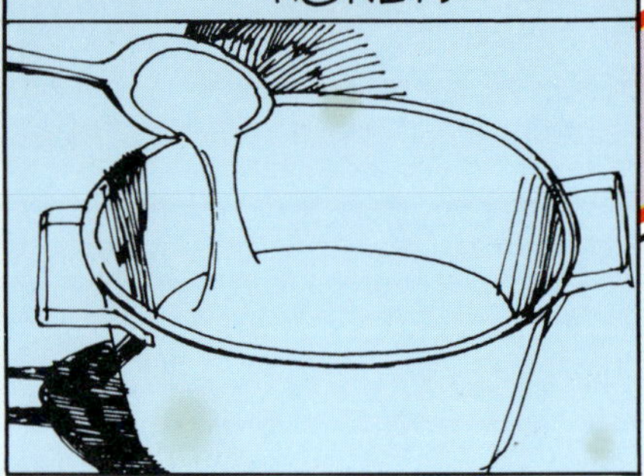

6. POUR THIS MIXTURE IN BOWL. MIX IN PEANUTS AND POPCORN.

7. SPREAD COATED CORN IN 2 LARGE CAKE PANS.

8. BAKE AT 350° FOR 10 TO 12 MINUTES. STIR ONCE WHILE COOKING.

9. COOL BEFORE SERVING FOR CRISPNESS. STORE EXTRA IN REFRIGERATOR.

# SUPER SUGGESTION

## MAKING POPCORN BALLS

First, let the Crack-a-joke mixture cool to room temperature. Then grease your hands with butter so the popcorn won't stick to them. Grab a handful of the mix and squeeze it hard into a ball.

# WONDER WOMAN'S NATURAL SODA POP

**FOOD YOU NEED:**

1 Can Frozen Fruit Juice Concentrate

Carbonated Water (like mineral water, club soda, or seltzer)

**TOOLS YOU NEED:**

Small Bowl

Fork

Large Bottle (28 ounces)

Funnel

Chopstick

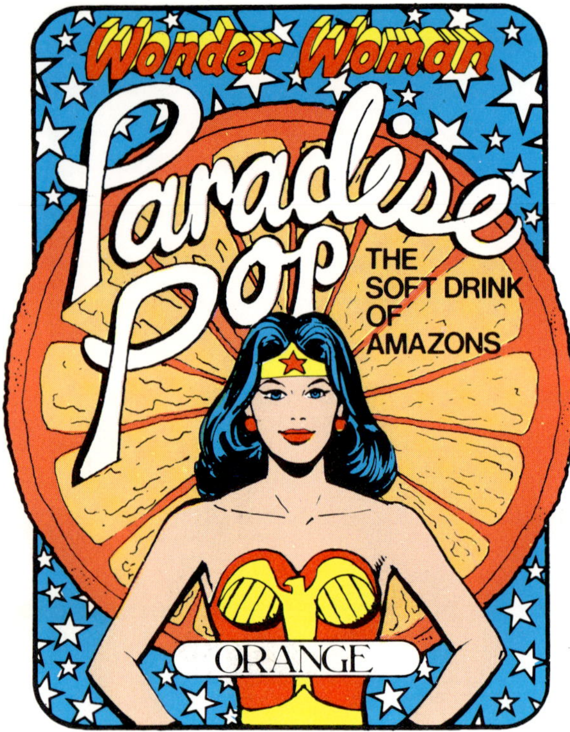


Ingredients: Carbonated water, natural fruit juice.

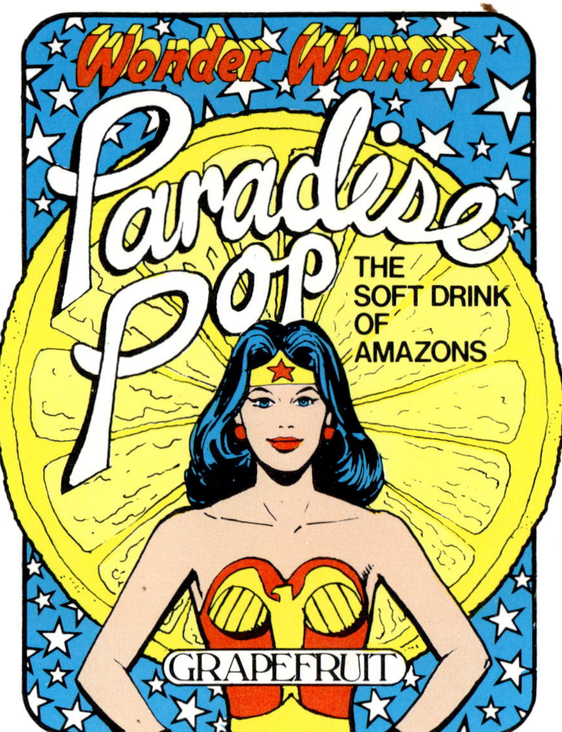


Ingredients: Carbonated water, natural fruit juice.

GREEN ARROW'S FRUIT SNACKS
NOW IF YOU STOP SHAKING, YOU'LL BE FINE. JUST TELL YOURSELVES...OR SHOULD I SAY WILLIAM TELL YOURSELVES... THAT YOU'RE TAKING PART IN THE CREATION OF A GREAT NEW FRUIT SNACK.
O.K. STAND STILL. READY... AIM...

# FIRE!

**TOOLS YOU NEED:**

Paring Knife
Cutting Board
Plastic Straws
Scissors
Green Paper (or White Paper colored green)

**FOOD YOU NEED:**

Any of the following—
Apple, Banana, Orange
Pineapple (fresh or canned)
Strawberries, Melon, Pear
Triangles of Cheese

1. WASH FRUIT AND CUT INTO BITE-SIZE PIECES.

2. PUSH STRAW THROUGH PIECES OF FRUIT. IF FRUIT IS TOO HARD, CUT HOLE WITH KNIFE.

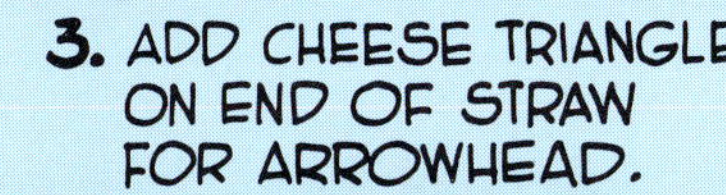


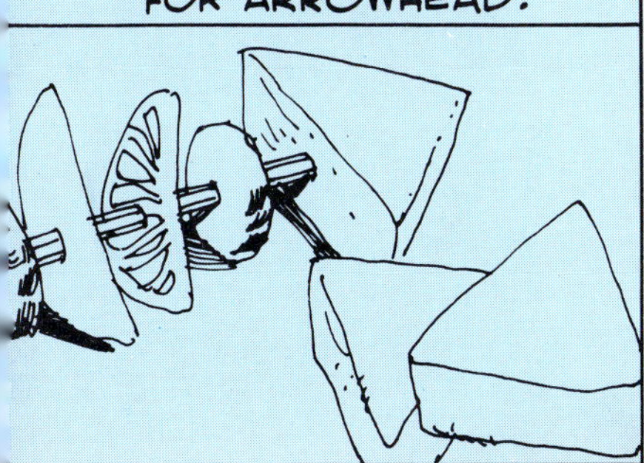

4. WITH SCISSORS, CUT A ½ INCH SLIT ON OTHER END. MAKE A GREEN PAPER FEATHER (*like the one in picture*) INSERT IN SLIT ON END OF STRAW.

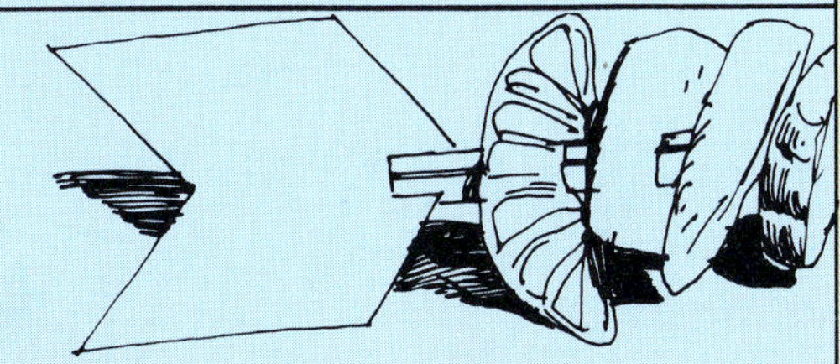

## OTHER QUICK FRUIT SNACKS

Fruits are a quick and easy snack, and there are a lot of different ways to eat them. Here are just a few—

**APPLES:**

- Cut into slices and spread each slice with peanut butter.
- Cut into slices, dip slices into orange or pineapple juice, and then into shredded coconut or chopped nuts.
- Make applesauce. Just peel an apple and cut it into chunks (leaving the core). Put chunks into blender with ½ teaspoon cinnamon. Push "puree" button.

**BANANAS:**

- Baked bananas. Peel one banana and cut in half lengthwise. Put in baking pan. Sprinkle each half with cinnamon and add a few very small pieces of butter. Cover pan with aluminum foil. Bake at 325° for 20 minutes.

**RAISINS:**

- Make a raisin mix with sunflower seeds, peanuts and sesame seeds.
- Have some raisins mixed with cottage cheese or yogurt.

# LOIS LANE'S PARTY VEGGIES AND DIP

**FOOD YOU NEED:**
(for dip)
½ Cup Shelled Sunflower Seeds
⅔ Cup Cottage Cheese
⅓ Cup Yogurt
¼ Cup Sesame Seeds

**TOOLS YOU NEED:**
Measuring Cup
Blender

**FOOD YOU NEED:**
(for dipping)
Celery, Carrots, Broccoli, Cauliflower, Cherry Tomatoes, Green Peppers
Any Other Raw Vegetables (except potatoes)

**TOOLS YOU NEED:**
Vegetable Knife
Cutting Board
Large Plate
Small Bowl

THANKS FOR THE PARTY, LOIS! THIS VEGETABLE DIP OF YOURS IS DELICIOUS. IS IT HARD TO MAKE?
OH, NOT AT ALL, PERRY. YOU JUST DO TO THE VEGETABLES WHAT YOU USUALLY DO TO MY STORIES. CUT THEM TO PIECES!

MEANWHILE, BACK IN LOIS'S KITCHEN, A BIZARRE SCENE UNFOLDS...
ATTENTION, JUNK FOOD EATERS. WE ARE THE VEGETABLE ROBOTS.
WE COME TO DESTROY JUNK FOOD!

WE WILL ANNIHILATE YOUR PUNY SUGAR-COATED SNACKS!

DO NOT TRY TO RESIST US. WE HAVE THE POWER OF NUTRIENTS.

TAKE US TO YOUR EATER!

1. WASH VEGETABLES AND PEEL IF NECESSARY.

2. CUT VEGETABLES INTO ROBOT SHAPES. SEE PHOTO FOR IDEAS.

3. ATTACH VEGETABLES TO EACH OTHER WITH TOOTHPICKS.

# SUPERMAN'S FROZEN FORTRESS POPS

**FOOD YOU NEED:**
(Serves 4–6)
2 Cups Orange Juice
6 Tablespoons Yogurt

**TOOLS YOU NEED:**
Measuring Cup
Measuring Spoons
Blender or Covered Jar
Popsicle Molds or Paper Cups
Popsicle Sticks

HEY, THOSE LOOK LIKE THE FROZEN YOGURT POPS YOU GAVE ME BEFORE. WHY DO YOU HAVE TO LEAVE THEM OUT HERE TO FREEZE?

SUPERGIRL, I CAN FLY FASTER THAN SOUND AND LIFT MOUNTAINS WITH ONE HAND. BUT I JUST CAN'T GET THE POWER COMPANY TO RUN A LINE UP HERE AND TURN ON MY REFRIGERATOR.

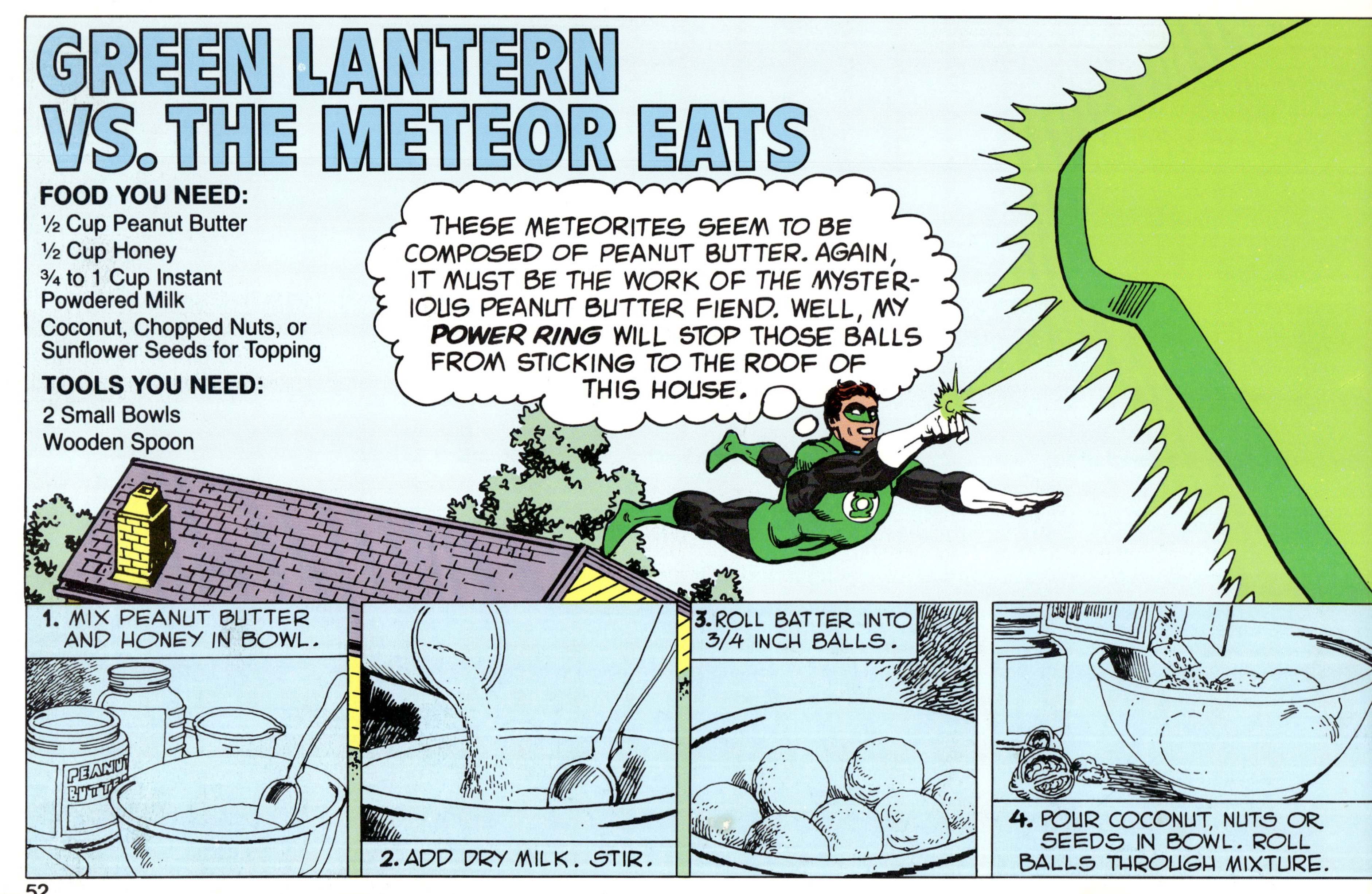
GREEN LANTERN VS. THE METEOR EATS
FOOD YOU NEED:
½ Cup Peanut Butter
½ Cup Honey
¾ to 1 Cup Instant Powdered Milk
Coconut, Chopped Nuts, or Sunflower Seeds for Topping
TOOLS YOU NEED:
2 Small Bowls
Wooden Spoon
THESE METEORITES SEEM TO BE COMPOSED OF PEANUT BUTTER. AGAIN, IT MUST BE THE WORK OF THE MYSTERIOUS PEANUT BUTTER FIEND. WELL, MY POWER RING WILL STOP THOSE BALLS FROM STICKING TO THE ROOF OF THIS HOUSE.
1. MIX PEANUT BUTTER AND HONEY IN BOWL.
2. ADD DRY MILK. STIR.
3. ROLL BATTER INTO 3/4 INCH BALLS.
4. POUR COCONUT, NUTS OR SEEDS IN BOWL. ROLL BALLS THROUGH MIXTURE.

5. REFRIGERATE 1 HOUR, THEN EAT. STORE LEFT-OVERS IN A COVERED CONTAINER IN REFRIGERATOR.

# MAIN MEALS

For some people it's lunchtime, for others it's dinner—that one time of day when you have your main meal. This meal should not only have a lot of food, it should also have a lot of nutrition. This section will give you some recipes for putting meals together. There are main courses, like chicken or hamburgers, and also salad, salad dressings, and vegetables. You can try cooking an entire meal, or you can help your father or mother in the kitchen by preparing one dish for a big meal.

If you're going to prepare one of the dishes in this section, it's a good idea to read the recipe the day before you start cooking. Check to see if you have all the ingredients you need, and also check how much time you'll need for cooking. Find out how many people you'll be cooking for, too. Most of the recipes in this section will feed four people.

And if you decide to put together a whole meal, make sure you include vegetables or a salad on the menu. You'll find a couple of new ideas for vegetable dishes in this section. You can pick the one that will go best with the main course you've decided to cook.

Want to add a dessert to your menu? Pick a fruit recipe from the snack section—it'll be a good dessert with any meal.

GLUP

# PERRY WHITE'S GREAT CAESAR'S SALAD

**FOOD YOU NEED:**

One or More of the Following:

Romaine Lettuce
Iceberg Lettuce
Bibb or Boston Lettuce
Raw Spinach Escarole
(use about 1 cup per person)

Also Choose Any of the Following.

Mushrooms, Cherry Tomatoes, Avocado, Cucumber, Sprouts, Carrots

**TOOLS YOU NEED:**

Colander
Cutting Board
Paring Knife
Salad Bowl
Toothpicks

1. TEAR OFF AMOUNT OF LETTUCE NEEDED. WASH EACH LEAF.

2. PLACE WASHED LETTUCE IN COLANDER TO DRAIN.

3. WASH AND CUT UP OTHER VEGETABLES TO BE ADDED.

4. RIP LETTUCE INTO BITE-SIZE PIECES. PLACE IN BOWL. ADD CUT-UP VEGETABLES.

5. BEFORE SERVING, POUR ON 1/4 CUP OR MORE OF SALAD DRESSING. MIX WELL.

6. TO MAKE *"DAILY PLANETS"*, CUT CHERRY TOMATO IN HALF, INSERT SLICE OF CUCUMBER, HOLD TOGETHER WITH TOOTHPICK.

SO THIS IS YOUR FAMOUS GREAT CAESAR'S SALAD. I NOTICE YOU'VE INCLUDED LITTLE DAILY PLANET EMBLEMS... VERY CLEVER. I NEVER KNEW YOU WERE SUCH A GREAT CHEF.
OLSEN, HOW MANY TIMES DO I HAVE TO TELL YOU, DON'T CALL ME CHEF!
AND DON'T EAT THE TOOTHPICKS!

2. COVER TIGHTLY AND SHAKE WELL.

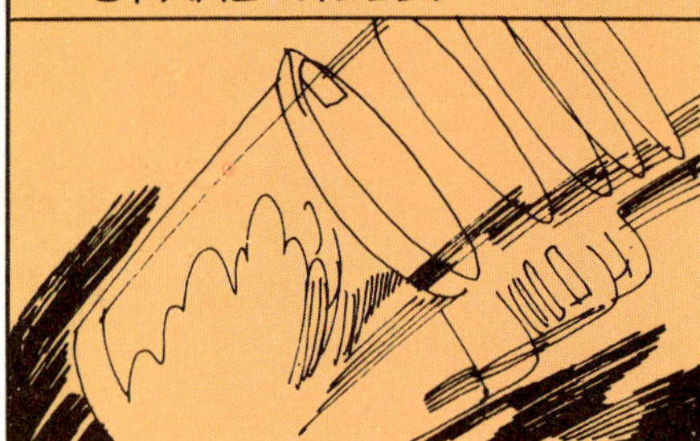

3. USE ½ CUP OR LESS OF DRESSING FOR A FAMILY SIZE SALAD. STORE REST IN REFRIGERATOR.

# BATMAN AND ROBIN'S

GEE, AFTER TELLING ROBIN SO MANY TIMES TO BE CAREFUL WITH THE LAB EQUIPMENT, I'D HATE FOR HIM TO SEE THAT I'M SITTING HERE MAKING SALAD DRESSING. I'D BETTER MAKE SURE HE'S NOT GETTING SUSPICIOUS.

## BATMAN'S DRESSING

**FOOD YOU NEED:**

⅔ Cup Vegetable Oil
3 Tablespoons Lemon Juice or Vinegar
One or All of the Following:
¼ Teaspoon Salt
¼ Teaspoon Basil
¼ Teaspoon Oregano
¼ Teaspoon Thyme

**TOOLS YOU NEED:**

Measuring Cup
Measuring Spoons
Jar with Lid

# SECRET SALAD DRESSINGS

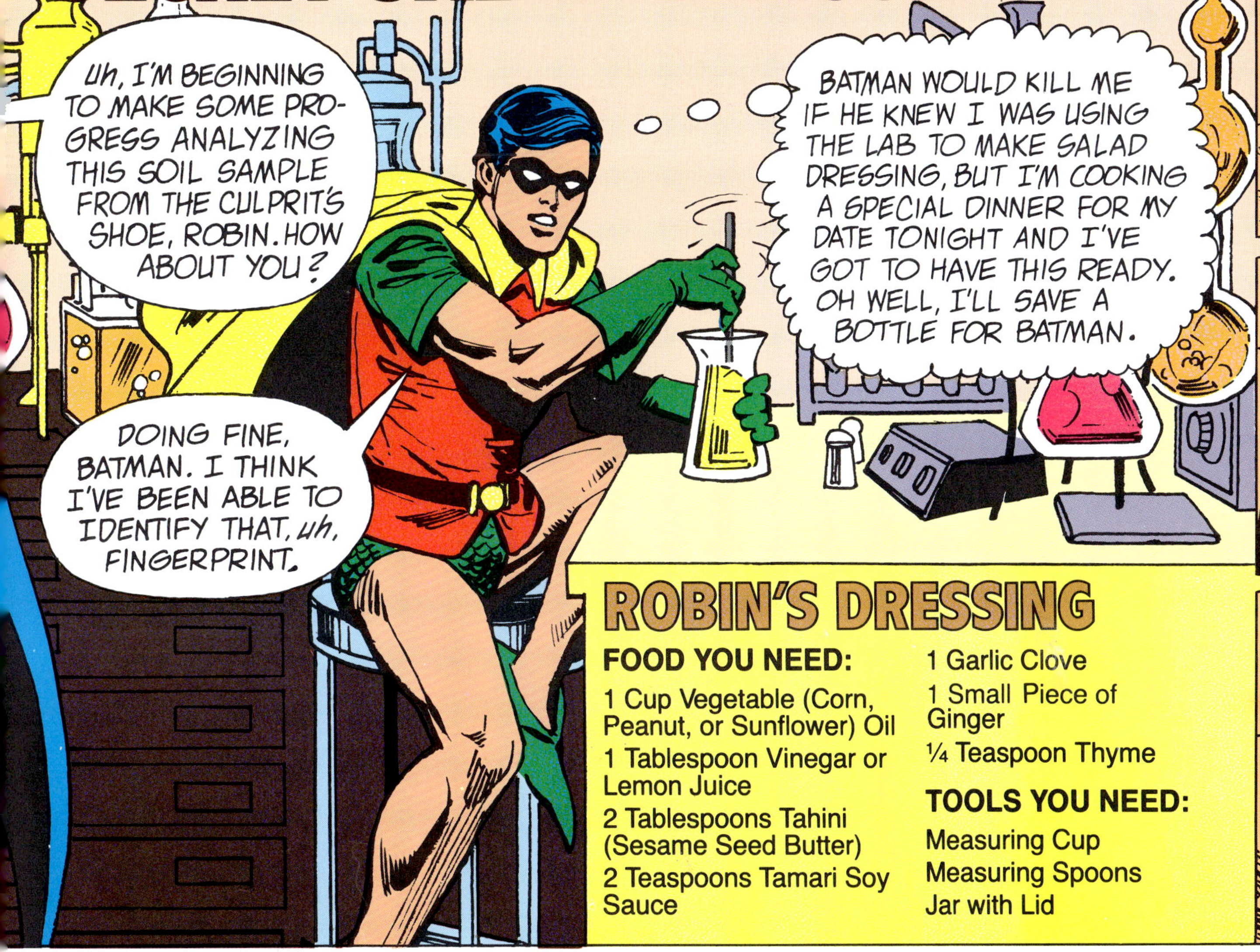

*Uh*, I'M BEGINNING TO MAKE SOME PROGRESS ANALYZING THIS SOIL SAMPLE FROM THE CULPRIT'S SHOE, ROBIN. HOW ABOUT YOU?

DOING FINE, BATMAN. I THINK I'VE BEEN ABLE TO IDENTIFY THAT, *uh*, FINGERPRINT.

BATMAN WOULD KILL ME IF HE KNEW I WAS USING THE LAB TO MAKE SALAD DRESSING, BUT I'M COOKING A SPECIAL DINNER FOR MY DATE TONIGHT AND I'VE GOT TO HAVE THIS READY. OH WELL, I'LL SAVE A BOTTLE FOR BATMAN.

## ROBIN'S DRESSING

**FOOD YOU NEED:**

1 Cup Vegetable (Corn, Peanut, or Sunflower) Oil
1 Tablespoon Vinegar or Lemon Juice
2 Tablespoons Tahini (Sesame Seed Butter)
2 Teaspoons Tamari Soy Sauce
1 Garlic Clove
1 Small Piece of Ginger
1/4 Teaspoon Thyme

**TOOLS YOU NEED:**

Measuring Cup
Measuring Spoons
Jar with Lid

**1.** PEEL THE CLOVE OF GARLIC AND PIECE OF GINGER.

**2.** PUT ALL INGREDIENTS INTO JAR, CLOSE THE LID TIGHTLY. SHAKE WELL.

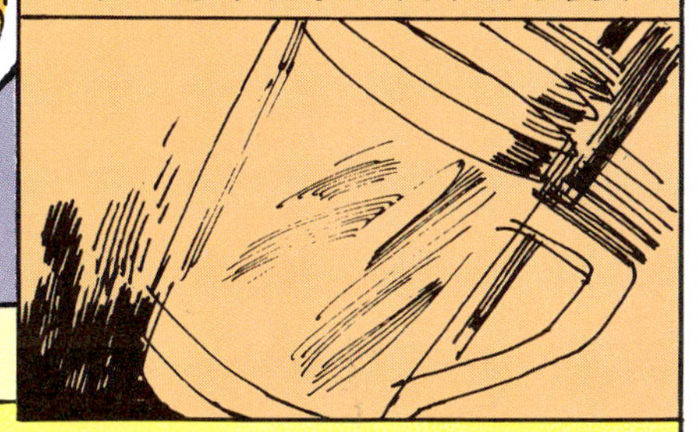

**3.** POUR ON SALAD. USE 1/2 CUP OR LESS FOR LARGE SALAD. WHEN POURING, DO NOT LET GARLIC OR GINGER FALL IN SALAD.

# "MY SECRET PIZZA" BY GREEN ARROW

**FOOD YOU NEED:**

4 Pita Breads
1 Quart or 4 Cups Tomato Sauce
16 Ounces Mozzarella Cheese
¼ Teaspoon Oregano
¼ Teaspoon Basil
If You Want, Add Any of the Following—
Sliced Onion, Green Pepper, Zucchini Slices, Parmesan Cheese, Sliced Mushrooms, or Minced Garlic

**TOOLS YOU NEED:**

Sharp Knife or Kitchen Scissors (make sure they're clean)
Spoon
Grater
Baking Pan or Cookie Sheet

450°
1. TURN OVEN TO 450°. CUT CIRCLES OUT OF PITA BREAD WITH KNIFE OR KITCHEN SCISSORS. BE CAREFUL NOT TO CUT THROUGH OTHER SIDE.
2. SPREAD TOMATO SAUCE ON BREAD WITH SPOON.

**3.** GRATE CHEESE AND PUT IT ON TOP OF SAUCE.

**4.** SPRINKLE PIES EVENLY WITH BASIL AND OREGANO.

**5.** IF YOU WANT, ADD ANY OF THE EXTRA TOPPINGS LISTED AT BEGINNING OF RECIPE.

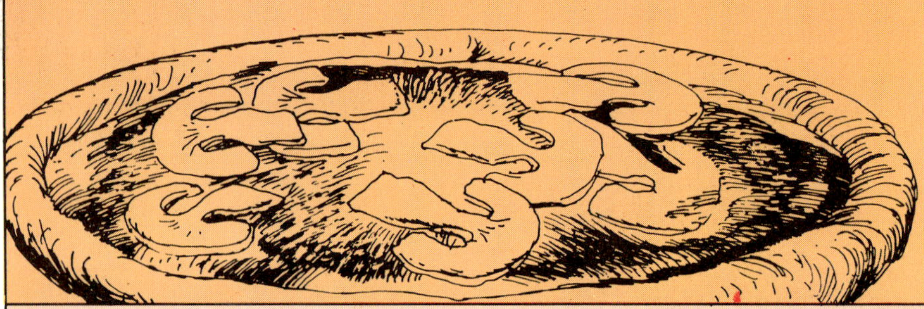

**6.** PUT PIES IN BAKING PAN OR ON COOKIE SHEET. BAKE 20-25 MINUTES, UNTIL CHEESE MELTS.

**7.** TO MAKE COVERS; LIGHTLY TOAST PITA BREAD CIRCLES IN TOASTER OR OVEN AND PLACE ON TOP OF COOKED PIZZA.

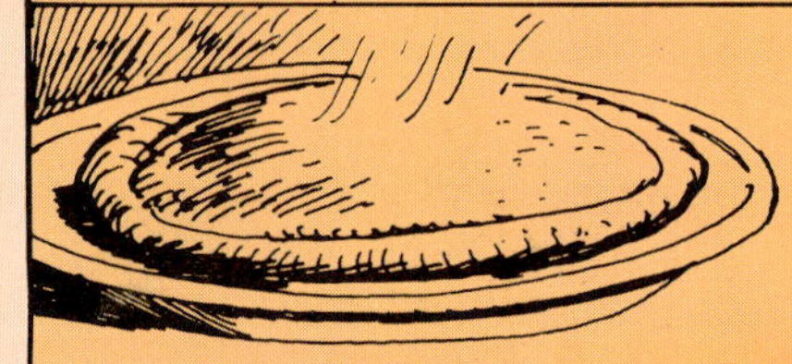

# SUPER SUGGESTION

## SETTING THE TABLE

As long as you're taking the trouble to cook a main meal, you might as well serve it on a table that looks good. Setting the table is not complicated. This picture shows a pretty simple way to do it. The fork goes on the left side and the knife and spoon go on the right, according to the rules of etiquette. This tradition probably got started because most people are right handed, so the knife was placed where the right hand can easily reach it. Now, this is the correct way to set the table, both for righties and lefties.

# PLASTIC MAN'S SPAGHETTI & MEATBALLS

**FOOD YOU NEED:**

For Spaghetti Sauce—
3 Tablespoons Vegetable Oil
1 Medium Onion
1 Clove Garlic
1 Can Tomato Puree (28 oz.)
1 Can Whole Tomatoes (28 oz.)
1 Teaspoon Oregano
1 Teaspoon Basil
1 Teaspoon Salt

For Meatballs—
2 Slices Whole Wheat Bread
½ Cup Water
¾ Pound Chopped Meat
2 Tablespoons Parmesan Cheese
1 Egg
½ Teaspoon Salt
¼ Teaspoon Oregano
3 Tablespoons Vegetable Oil

For Spaghetti—
1 Pound Spaghetti (Whole Wheat, High Protein, or Green Spinach)
1 Tablespoon Vegetable Oil

**TOOLS YOU NEED:**

Large Pot
Sharp Knife
Wooden Spoon
Fork
Mixing Bowl
Large Frying Pan

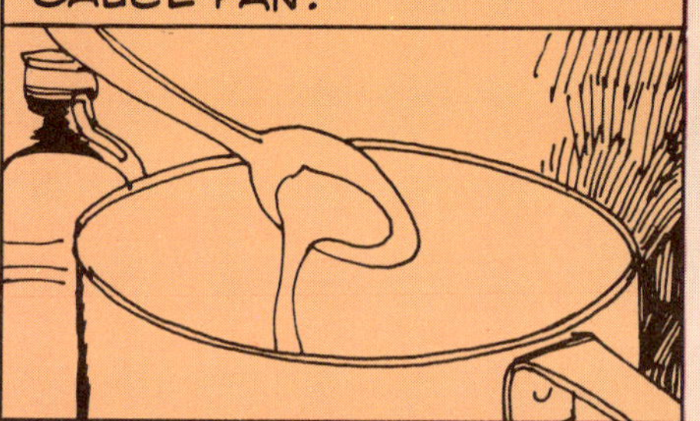

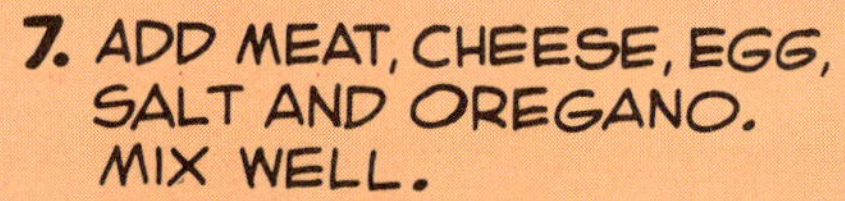

9. PUT 3TBS. OIL INTO FRYING PAN. HEAT ON MEDIUM FLAME.

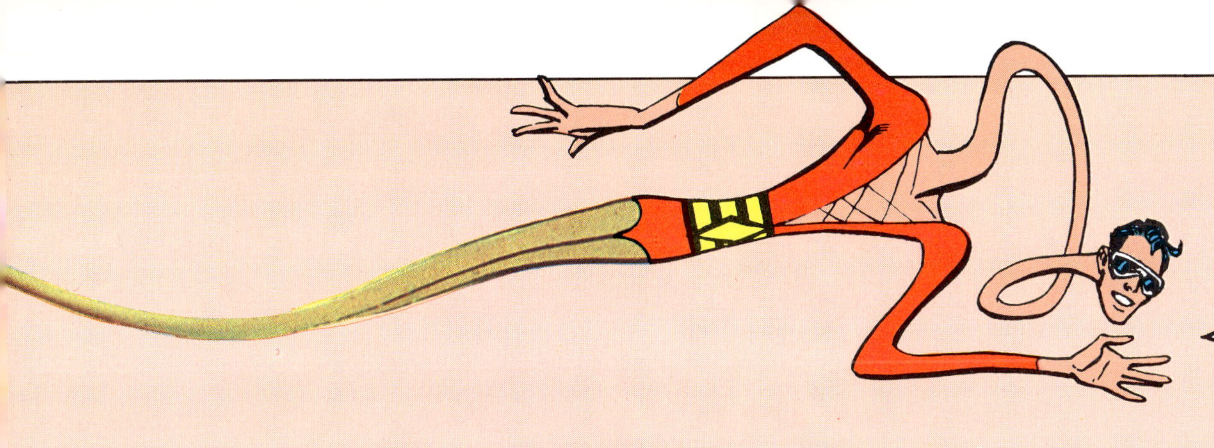


3. PUT CUT UP ONION AND GARLIC INTO SAUCE PAN. HEAT ON LOW FLAME TILL ONIONS ARE CLEAR AND SOFT.

4. ADD TOMATO PUREE, TOMATOES, AND SPICES. STIR WITH WOODEN SPOON.

5. COOK ON LOW FLAME AT LEAST 30 MINUTES, WHILE YOU MAKE MEATBALLS.

6. TO MAKE MEATBALLS, PUT BREAD AND WATER INTO BOWL. MASH WITH FORK OR CLEAN HANDS.

10. WITH SPOON, CAREFULLY PLACE MEATBALLS IN PAN.

11. COOK 2 MINUTES, THEN TURN MEATBALLS WITH SPOON. COOK TILL BROWN ON ALL SIDES.

12. REMOVE MEATBALLS AND PLACE THEM IN SPAGHETTI SAUCE. COOK 15 MINUTES.

13. TO MAKE SPAGHETTI, FOLLOW THE DIRECTIONS ON THE PACKAGE. TO PREVENT SPAGHETTI FROM STICKING TOGETHER, TRY PUTTING A TABLESPOON OF VEGETABLE OIL INTO THE WATER WHILE SPAGHETTI IS COOKING.

# COMMISSIONER GORDON'S UNDERCOVER VEGETABLES

1. WASH AND CUT UP 3 CUPS VEGETABLES AND PUT INTO BAG. POUR 1TBS. OIL INTO BAG.

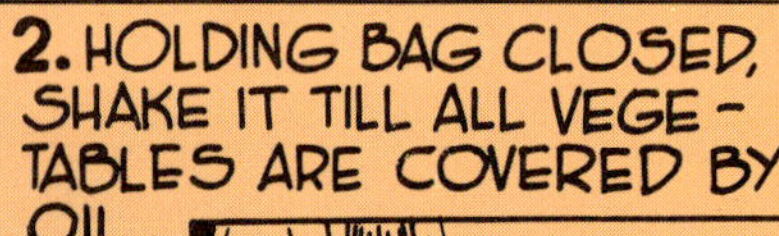

2. HOLDING BAG CLOSED, SHAKE IT TILL ALL VEGETABLES ARE COVERED BY OIL.

**FOOD YOU NEED:**
(serves 4)

3 Cups Mixed Fresh Vegetables: Carrots, Broccoli, Mushrooms, Cauliflower, String Beans, Green Peppers

1 Tablespoon Vegetable Oil

½ Cup Breadcrumbs or Wheat Germ

¼ Teaspoon Salt

1 Teaspoon Vegetable Oil

**TOOLS YOU NEED:**

Measuring Cup
Measuring Spoons
Large Plastic Bag
Oven Pan
Paper Towel or Napkin
Aluminum Foil
Paring Knife

I'M COMMISSIONER GORDON. YOU VEGETABLES HAVE BEEN PICKED FOR AN IMPORTANT MISSION. YOU ARE GOING TO GET PEOPLE WHO NEVER TOUCHED VEGETABLES TO TASTE YOU AND LEARN TO LOVE YOU. FOR THIS, THE BATMAN AND I HAVE DEVISED THIS ELABORATE DISGUISE!
WHILE UNDERCOVER, YOU WILL EASILY PASS INTO THE VICTIM'S DINNER PLATE. WITHOUT KNOWING, THE VEGETABLE-HATER WILL TAKE A TASTE, AND WHEN HE FINDS OUT YOUR TRUE IDENTITY, IT WILL BE TOO LATE. HE WILL COME TO REALIZE YOUR BASIC YUMMINESS. GOOD LUCK, VEGETABLES!
3. ADD SALT AND BREAD CRUMBS TO BAG.
4. POUR 1 TSP. OF OIL INTO OVEN PAN. USE PAPER TOWEL TO SPREAD OIL ON BOTTOM OF PAN.
5. PUT SINGLE LAYER OF VEGETABLES IN PAN. COVER PAN WITH FOIL. BAKE AT 350° FOR 20-25 MINUTES.
350°

# FLASH'S SPEED-STIRRED VEGETABLES

**FOOD YOU NEED:**
(Serves 4)

1 Onion

4 Cups of Mixed Vegetables

Use any combination of—
Carrots, Broccoli, Peppers, Cauliflower, Peas, Mushrooms, Cabbage, Zucchini, Celery

1 Tablespoon Vegetable Oil

¼ Teaspoon Oregano

¼ Teaspoon Basil

¼ Teaspoon Salt

**TOOLS YOU NEED:**

Paring Knife
Measuring Spoons
Large Heavy Skillet or Frying Pan
Long Wooden Spoon

# THE ATOM'S SUPER HERO SANDWICH

**FOOD YOU NEED:**

1 Loaf Italian Bread (Long)
7 Ounces Tuna Fish (Large Can)
2 Tablespoons Mayonnaise
6 Slices Cheese (Swiss, Provolone, or Cheddar)
1 Cup Lettuce
1 Cup Tomato
1 Cup Green Pepper
½ Cup Sprouts
2 Teaspoons Vinegar
2 Teaspoons Vegetable Oil
Pinch of Basil
Pinch of Oregano

**TOOLS YOU NEED:**

Mixing Bowl
Fork
Bread Knife

1. PUT TUNA FISH AND MAYONNAISE IN BOWL. MIX WELL WITH FORK.

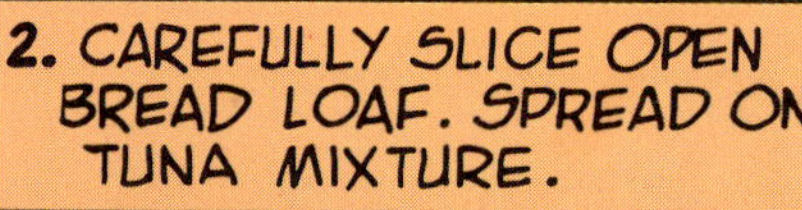

2. CAREFULLY SLICE OPEN BREAD LOAF. SPREAD ON TUNA MIXTURE.

3. ADD LETTUCE, TOMATO, PEPPER AND SPROUTS.

4. THEN SPRINKLE ON OIL, VINEGAR, BASIL, AND OREGANO.

5. CUT INTO AS MANY SLICES AS YOU WANT. YOU CAN ALSO TRY THIS SANDWICH WITH TURKEY BREAST OR SLICED CHICKEN INSTEAD OF TUNA.

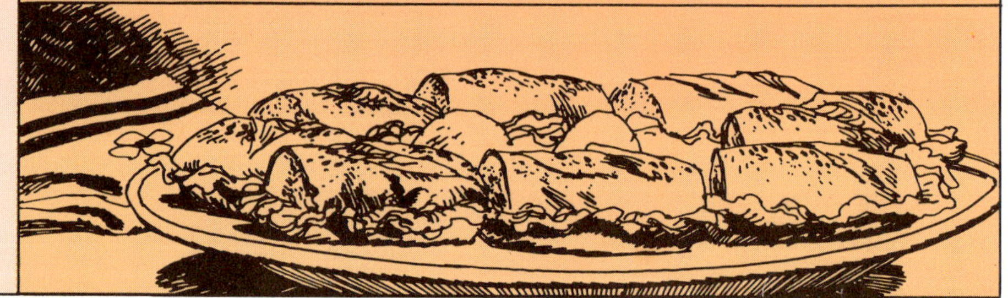

MILD MANNERED BURGER
THE PEOPLE WHO KNOW THIS HAMBURGER THINK OF IT AS JUST A MEEK, TIMID SORT OF FOOD, HIDING FROM THE WORLD BEHIND ITS PICKLE GLASSES. "NUTRITIOUS? THAT MEAT PATTIE?" THEY SCOFF, "WHY IT COULDN'T FEED A FLY!" BUT LITTLE DO THEY KNOW...

1. PUT BEEF, WHEAT GERM, TOMATO JUICE, MUSTARD AND SOY SAUCE IN BOWL. MIX WITH FORK.

2. FORM MEAT INTO SIX BALLS, THEN PRESS INTO PATTIES. DON'T PRESS HARD.

3. TO MAKE EMBLEMS: CUT CORNERS OFF SQUARE SLICES OF CHEESE, AS SHOWN:

4. PLACE PATTIES IN PAN AND BROIL IN OVEN FOR ABOUT 5 MINUTES.

5. FLIP PATTIES AND COOK FOR 5 MORE MINUTES. THEN PLACE CHEESE EMBLEMS ON TOP OF PATTIES.

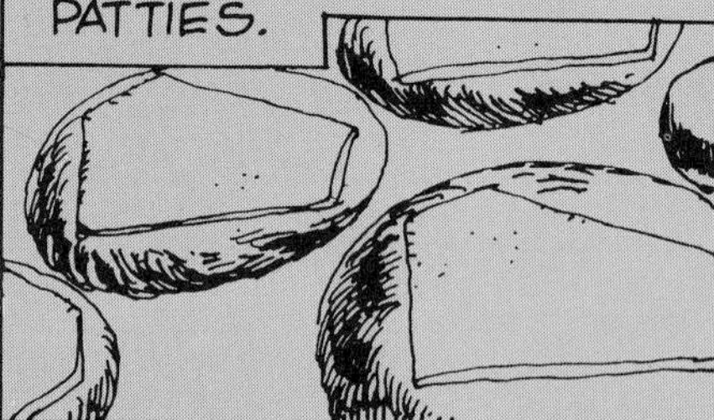

6. PUT BACK IN OVEN UNTIL CHEESE MELTS (ABOUT 1 MINUTE). WATCH CLOSELY SO THAT THEY DON'T BURN.

7. TOAST ROLLS OR MUFFINS, PUT HAMBURGERS INSIDE (CHEESE SIDE UP).

8. MAKE "S" ON EMBLEM WITH KETCHUP, AND ADD TOPPINGS OF YOUR CHOICE.

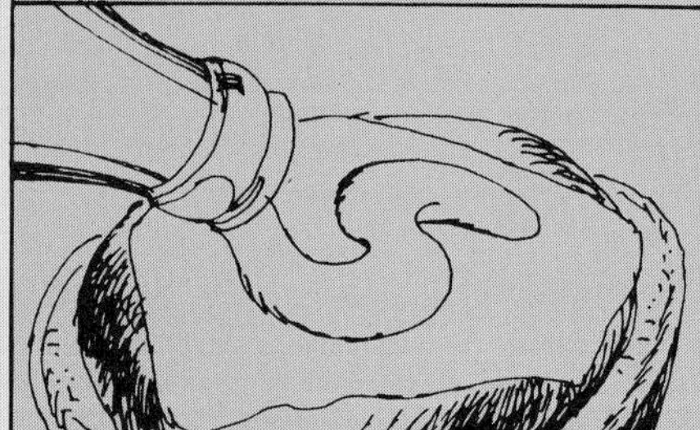

9. CLOSE BUN, CONSTRUCT EYEGLASSES WITH PICKLE SLICES AND TOOTHPICKS. USE RED PEPPER FOR MOUTH.

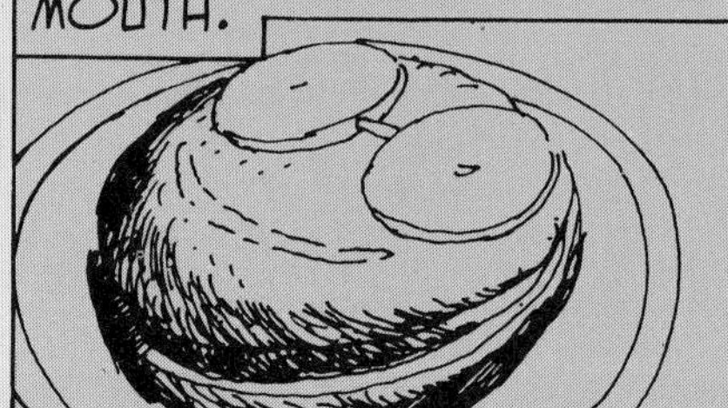

**FOOD YOU NEED:**
(Serves 4–6)

12 Ounces Ground Beef
¼ Cup Wheat Germ
½ Cup Bread Crumbs
½ Cup Tomato Juice
1 Teaspoon Mustard
½ Soy Sauce
6 Whole Wheat English Muffins or Rolls
Pickle Slices
Cheese
Tomato Ketchup

**TOOLS YOU NEED:**

Measuring Cup
Measuring Spoons
Medium Sized Bowl
Fork
Small Knife
Oven Pan
Toothpicks

...THAT BENEATH THAT SHY EXTERIOR, THIS BURGER HAS A SECRET IDENTITY (AS WELL AS SOME SECRET INGREDIENTS).

1. BREAK EGG INTO BOWL, ADD WATER AND BEAT WITH FORK.
2. IN ANOTHER BOWL, MIX WHEAT GERM, SALT, THYME AND MARJORAM.
3. DIP A PIECE OF CHICKEN INTO EGG AND WATER, COVER COMPLETELY WITH EGG.
4. ROLL IT IN WHEAT GERM MIXTURE, UNTIL COMPLETELY COVERED.
SUPERGIRL'S HEAT VISION CHICKEN
SSSSS!

**FOOD YOU NEED:**
(Serves 4)
1 Chicken, cut-up or quartered
1 Egg
¼ Cup Water
1 Cup Wheat Germ
½ Teaspoon Salt
¼ Teaspoon Marjoram
¼ Teaspoon Thyme

**TOOLS YOU NEED:**
Fork
2 Soup Bowls
Large Oven Pan

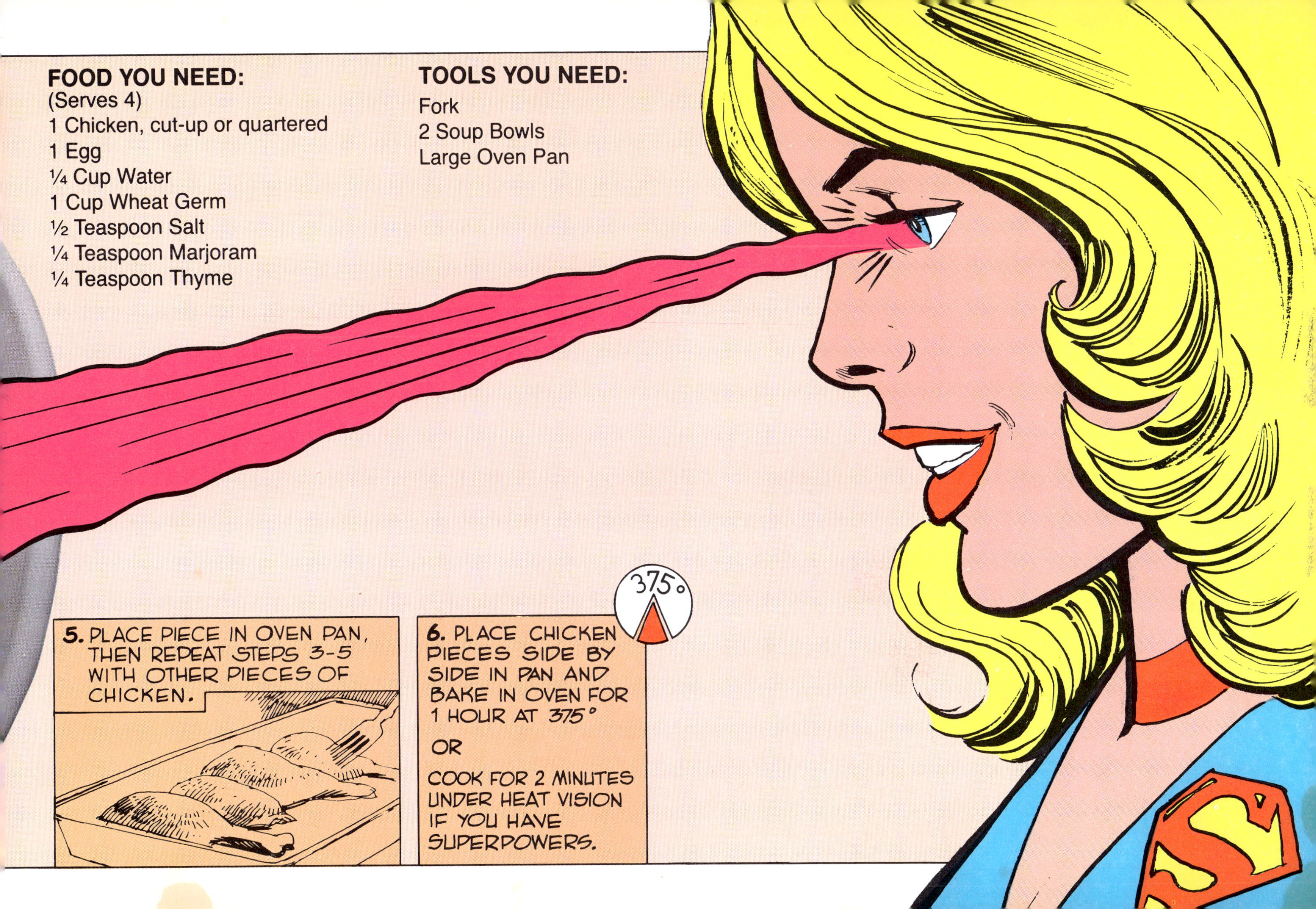

Food can be at its worst at parties. Sometimes, the only thing you can find to eat at a party are bowls of over-sweetened junk food and brown sugary liquids to wash it down with. But when you have *your* party, things are going to be different. In this section are recipes for your party that are nutritious. Some of the recipes do call for sugar, but it is a small amount, and it is combined with other ingredients containing nutrients. The food will still be great, the guests will love it, and you don't have to feel guilty about pushing too much sugar on them.

Most of these recipes will serve 12 kids. It's a good idea to start preparing the food a day or so before the party. You might not have time to make all the food in one day, and a recipe like the Brownie Ice Cream (p. 90) needs a lot of time to make.

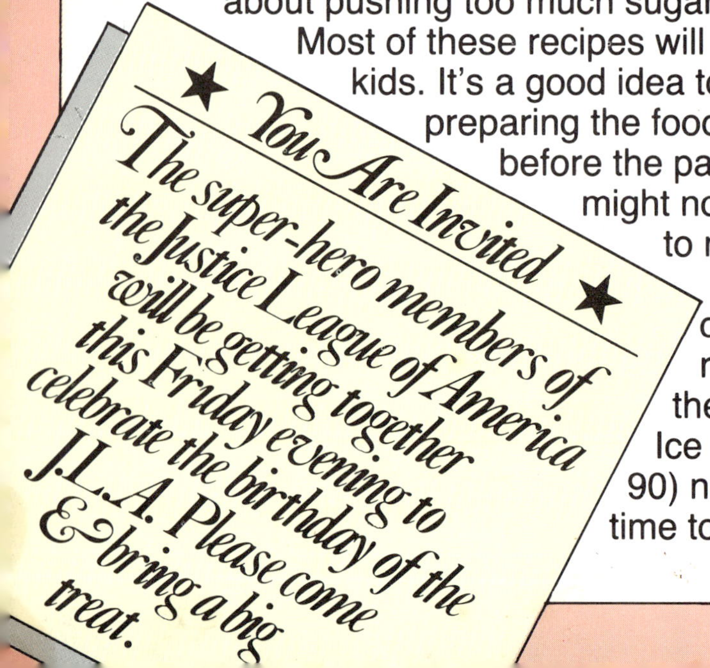

★ *You Are Invited* ★

*The super-hero members of the Justice League of America will be getting together this Friday evening to celebrate the birthday of the J.L.A. Please come & bring a big treat.*

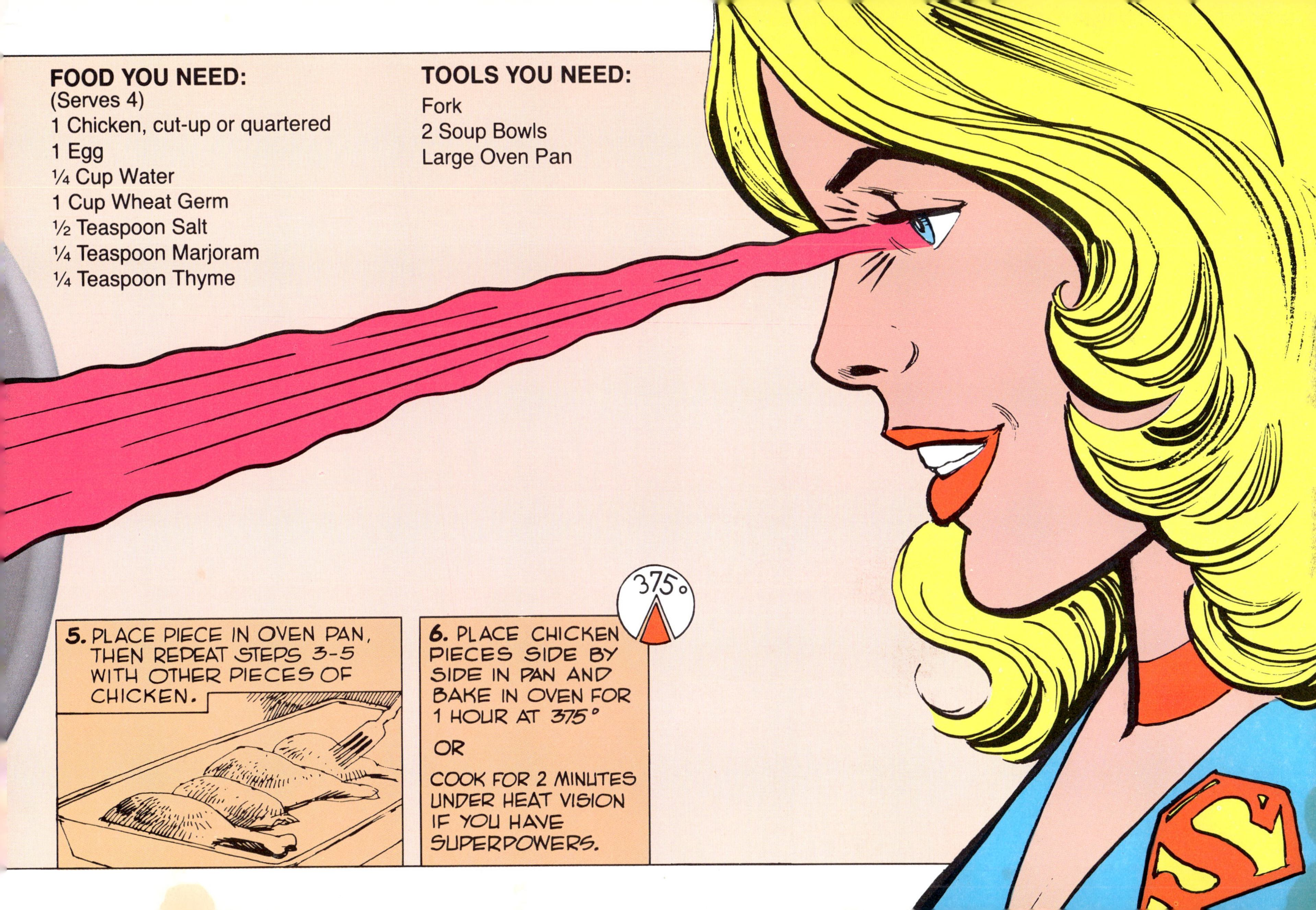


**FOOD YOU NEED:**
(Serves 4)
1 Chicken, cut-up or quartered
1 Egg
¼ Cup Water
1 Cup Wheat Germ
½ Teaspoon Salt
¼ Teaspoon Marjoram
¼ Teaspoon Thyme

**TOOLS YOU NEED:**
Fork
2 Soup Bowls
Large Oven Pan

Food can be at its worst at parties. Sometimes, the only thing you can find to eat at a party are bowls of over-sweetened junk food and brown sugary liquids to wash it down with. But when you have *your* party, things are going to be different. In this section are recipes for your party that are nutritious. Some of the recipes do call for sugar, but it is a small amount, and it is combined with other ingredients containing nutrients. The food will still be great, the guests will love it, and you don't have to feel guilty about pushing too much sugar on them.

Most of these recipes will serve 12 kids. It's a good idea to start preparing the food a day or so before the party. You might not have time to make all the food in one day, and a recipe like the Brownie Ice Cream (p. 90) needs a lot of time to make.

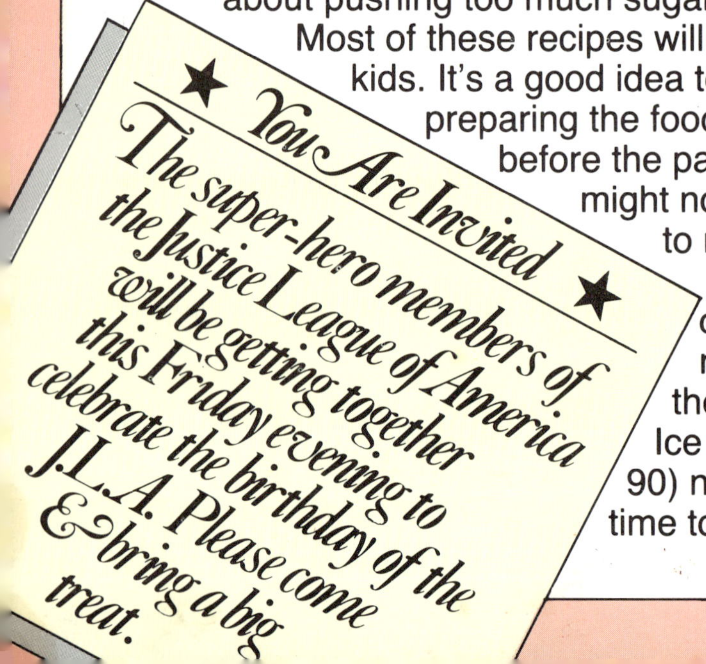

★ *You Are Invited* ★

*The super-hero members of the Justice League of America will be getting together this Friday evening to celebrate the birthday of the J.L.A. Please come & bring a big treat.*

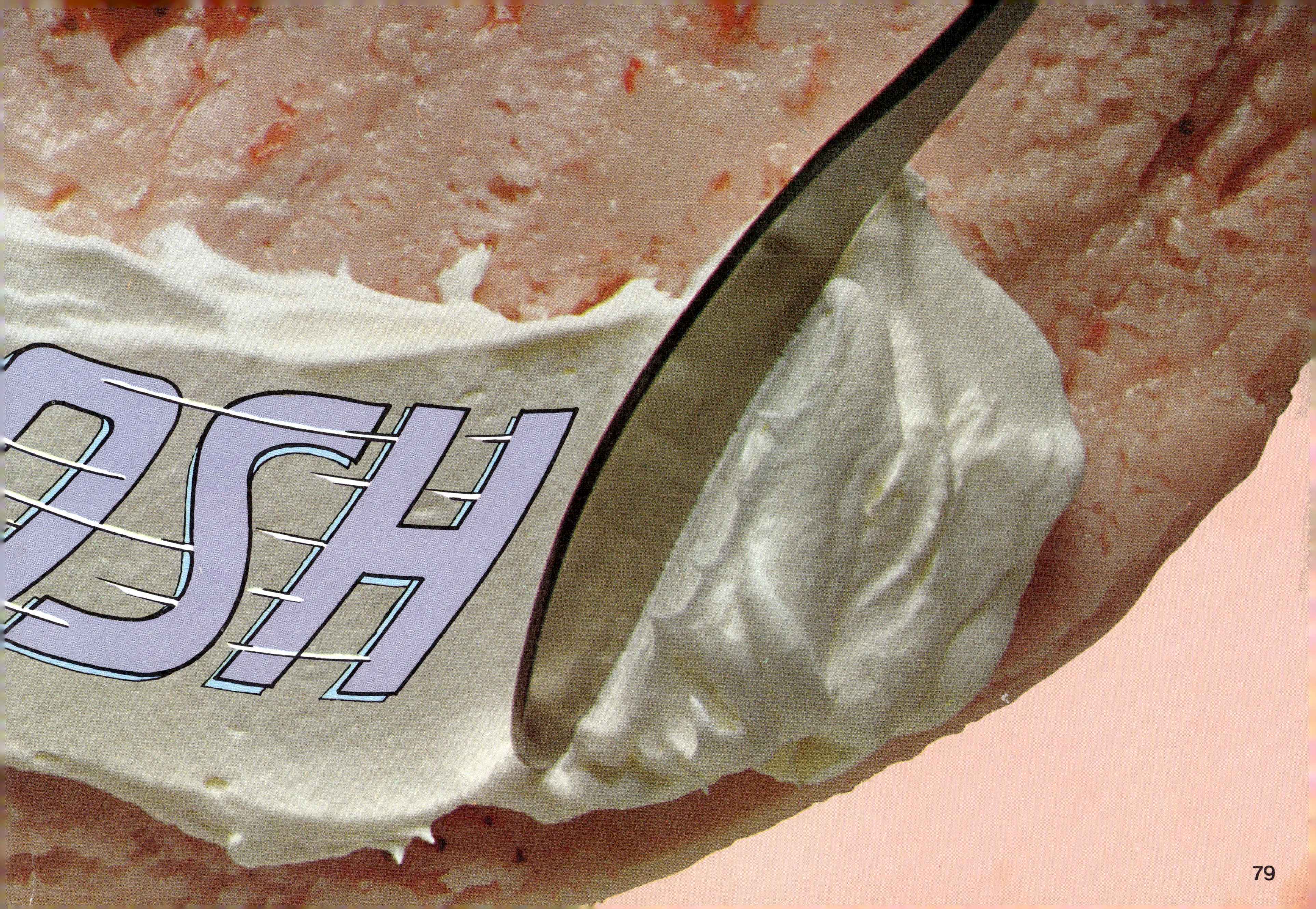

# GREEN LANTERN AND THE COOKIE PRINTS

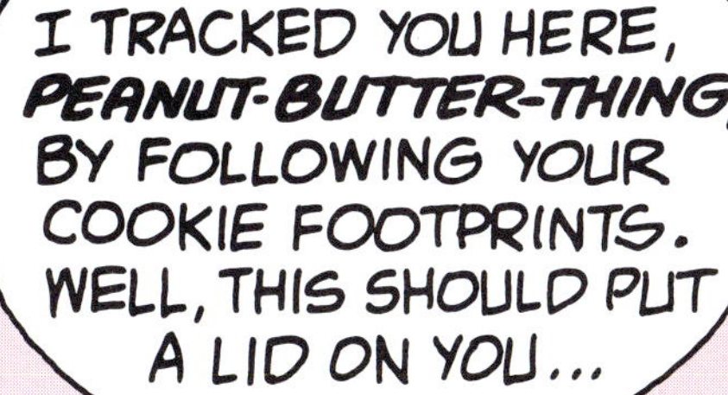

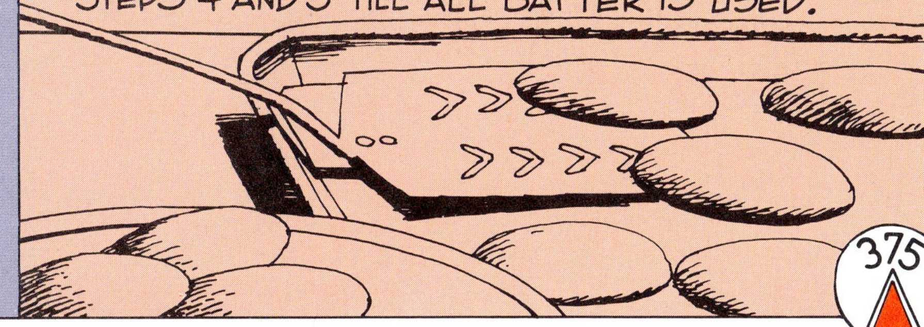

**TOOLS YOU NEED:**

Fork
Large Bowl
1 or 2 Cookie Sheets
2 Teaspoons
Spatula

**FOOD YOU NEED:**

(makes about 3 ½ dozen)
2 Ripe Bananas
½ Cup Vegetable Oil
⅔ Cup Brown Sugar
1 Egg
½ Cup Peanut Butter
⅔ Cup Oatmeal
1 ½ Cup Flour
½ Teaspoon Baking Soda
1 Teaspoon Cinnamon
½ Teaspoon Salt
Raisins or Nuts (if you want)

# THE ATOM'S KNOCKOUT PUNCH

**FOOD YOU NEED:**
(makes about 18 servings, 6 ounces each)

For Punch—

1 Large Can Pineapple Juice

1 Large Can or Bottle Apple Juice

1 Pound Strawberries (Fresh or Frozen—if using frozen berries, thaw 1 hour before starting recipe)

For Frozen Fruit Block:

1 Large Can Pineapple Juice

**TOOLS YOU NEED:**

Small Knife

Blender

Punch Bowl, Soup Pot, or Any Large Bowl

Long Spoon

1 Empty ½ Gallon Milk or Juice Container (for Frozen Fruit Block)

POW!
EVERYONE WHO'S TASTED MY STRAW-BERRY PUNCH SAYS IT'S A KNOCKOUT! AND THIS FROZEN FRUIT BLOCK SHOULD KEEP IT COLD UNTIL I GET IT TO THE PARTY. *Hmmm...* I GUESS THIS IS ONE WAY TO BLOCK A PUNCH!
1. TO MAKE PUNCH: CUT UP BERRIES AND PUT INTO BLENDER CUP. PUREE IN BLENDER.
2. OPEN PINEAPPLE AND APPLE JUICE. POUR INTO BOWL.
3. ADD PUREED STRAW-BERRIES AND STIR PUNCH WITH SPOON.

1. TO MAKE FROZEN BLOCK: WASH MILK OR JUICE CARTON THOROUGHLY. POUR JUICE INTO CARTON.

2. PUT INTO FREEZER TILL FROZEN (AT LEAST 4 HOURS).

3. WHEN READY TO SERVE, RIP OFF CARTON.

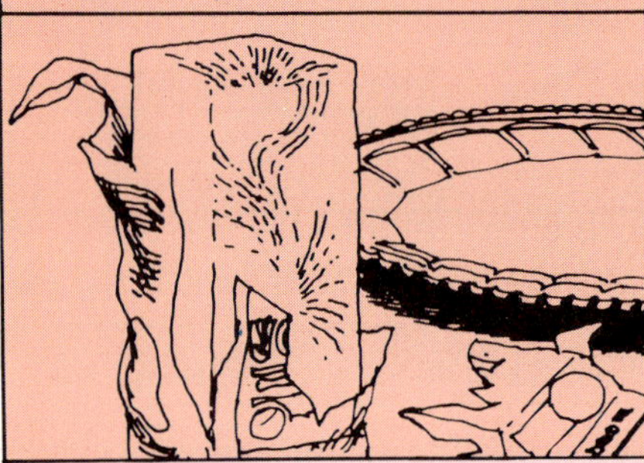

4. PUT ICE BLOCK INTO PUNCH BOWL. PUNCH WILL STAY COOL DURING PARTY.

## FRUIT CUBES

They're easy to make!

- Put a piece of fruit in each section of an ice cube tray.
- Pour *fruit juice* into tray.
- Carefully put tray into freezer.
- Wait at least an *hour*, then add cubes to punch, or put them in a tall glass and add fruit juice.

# SUPER SUGGESTION

## HOW TO BUY FRUIT JUICE

Pick up the can or bottle of fruit juice and look closely at the label. Does it say fruit JUICE or fruit DRINK? There's a big difference. Fruit drink is mostly water. There could be as little as 10% fruit juice in a can of fruit drink. The rest is water and sometimes sugar. If you check the ingredients, you'll see that. So fruit juice is really a better buy, because it's all juice inside the can.

# FLASH'S QUICK APPLE CRISP

Had to dash, but left this apple dish. Be back for the party in 1/1000th of a second! --Flash

**FOOD YOU NEED:**
(serves 8)
4–5 Apples
¾ Cup Flour
¾ Cup Brown Sugar
½ Teaspoon Cinnamon
½ Teaspoon Nutmeg
¼ Teaspoon Salt
⅓ Cup Melted Butter

**TOOLS YOU NEED:**
9″ Pie Pan
Medium Mixing Bowl
Wooden Spoon
Paring Knife
Small Saucepan

**1.** PEEL AND CUT UP APPLES. PUT PIECES IN PIE PAN.

**2.** PUT SALT, FLOUR, SUGAR, CINNAMON, NUTMEG IN BOWL. MELT BUTTER IN SAUCEPAN AND POUR IN BOWL. MIX WITH FORK.

**3.** SPOON MIXTURE OVER APPLES IN PAN, COVERING COMPLETELY. BAKE AT 375° FOR 35 MINUTES, OR UNTIL APPLES ARE SOFT.

375°

**4.** SERVE IN SMALL DESSERT DISHES. TRY TOPPING WITH VANILLA ICE CREAM OR WHIPPED CREAM.

# WONDER WOMAN'S ROCKET POPS

**FOOD YOU NEED:**
6 Bananas
3 Ounce Carob Bar
¼ Cup Water
¼ Cup Milk
½ Cup Coconut
½ Cup Wheat Germ
½ Cup Nuts

**TOOLS YOU NEED:**
12 Popsicle Sticks
Small Frying Pan or Pot
Wooden Spoon
4 Soup Bowls
Dinner Plate or Pan
Wax Paper

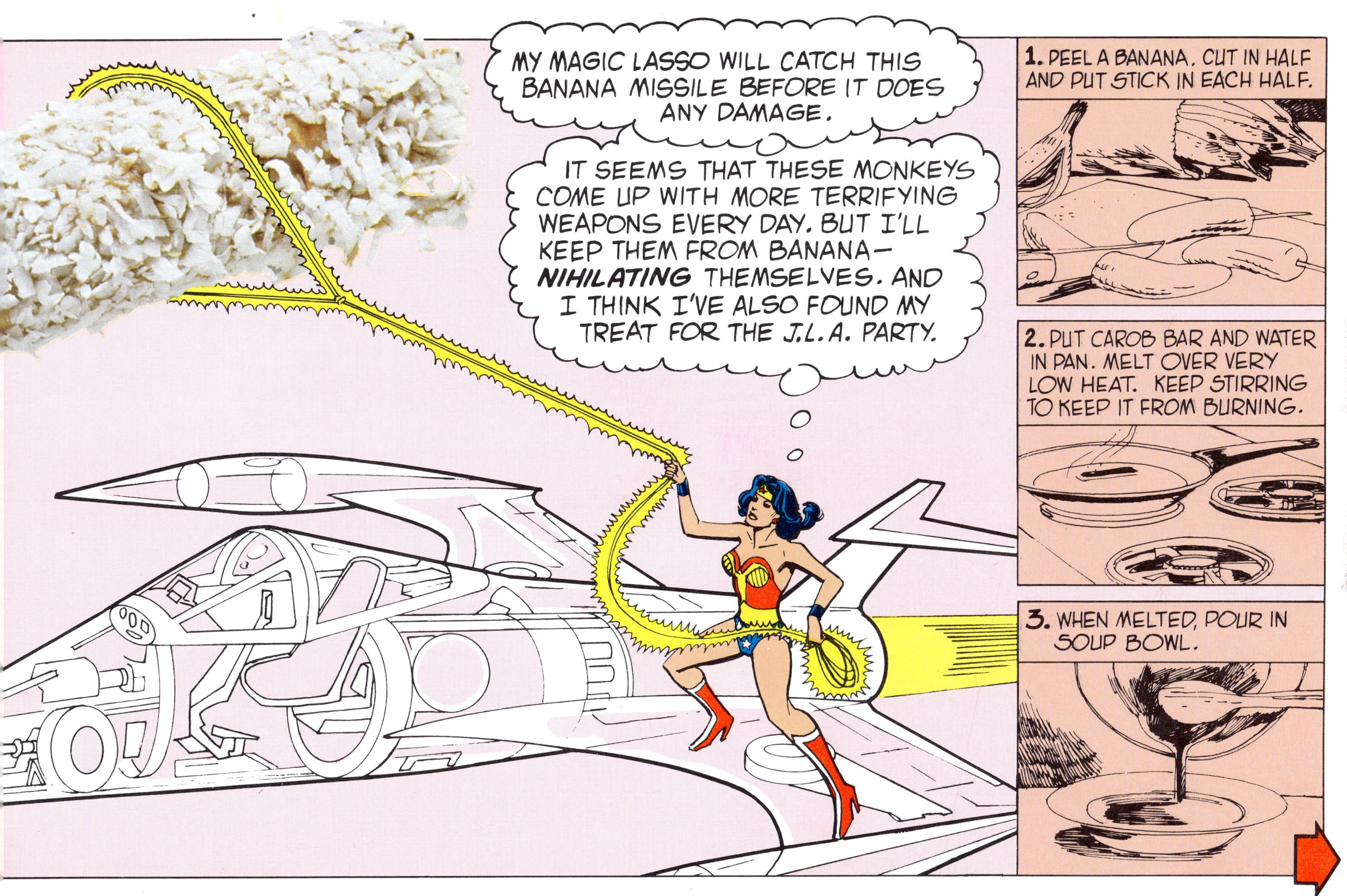
MY MAGIC LASSO WILL CATCH THIS BANANA MISSILE BEFORE IT DOES ANY DAMAGE.
IT SEEMS THAT THESE MONKEYS COME UP WITH MORE TERRIFYING WEAPONS EVERY DAY. BUT I'LL KEEP THEM FROM BANANA-*NIHILATING* THEMSELVES. AND I THINK I'VE ALSO FOUND MY TREAT FOR THE J.L.A. PARTY.
1. PEEL A BANANA. CUT IN HALF AND PUT STICK IN EACH HALF.
2. PUT CAROB BAR AND WATER IN PAN. MELT OVER VERY LOW HEAT. KEEP STIRRING TO KEEP IT FROM BURNING.
3. WHEN MELTED, POUR IN SOUP BOWL.

4. ADD MILK. STIR UNTIL SMOOTH.

5. PUT COCONUT, WHEAT GERM AND NUTS INTO SEPARATE BOWLS.

6. DIP BANANA HALVES INTO CAROB MIXTURE. COVER COMPLETELY. USE A SPOON TO HELP COVER THE WHOLE BANANA.

7. ROLL CAROB COVERED BANANA IN COCONUT, WHEAT GERM OR NUTS.

8. PUT BANANA ON PLATE COVERED WITH WAX PAPER. REPEAT STEPS 5, 6, AND 7 WITH REST OF BANANAS.

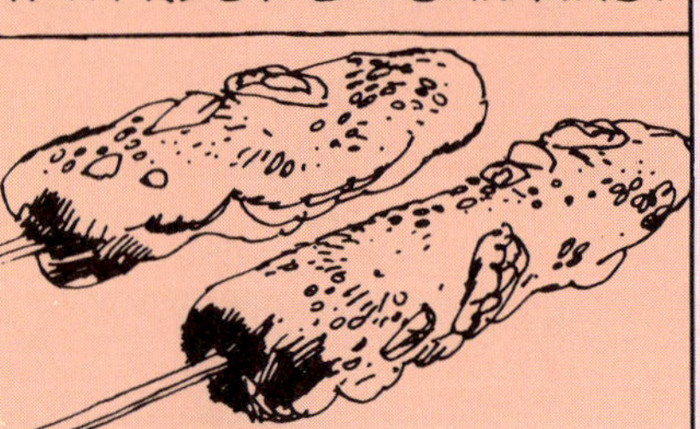

9. PUT IN FREEZER FOR A LEAST 2 HOURS. SERVE FROZEN.

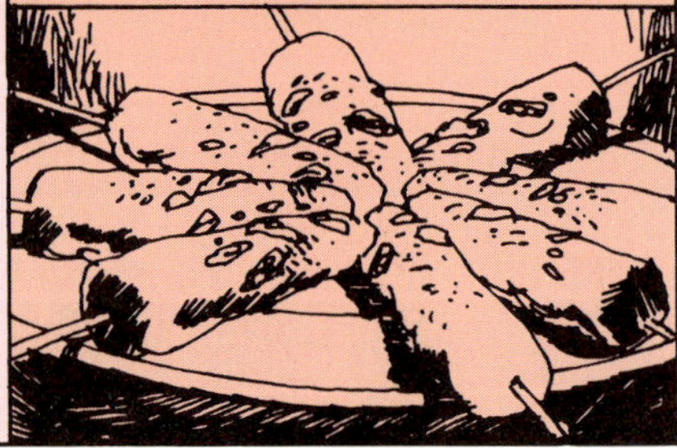

# SUPER SUGGESTION

## BANANA PARTY TRICK

**How it looks:**
You quiet down your party guests and hold up a banana. "Watch this!" you say, "I will use my super-powered banana-vision to slice this banana in its peel, without touching it." You stare at the banana, then slowly remove the peel, and to everyone's shock, the banana inside is sliced!

**How to do it:**
It's just a matter of preparing the banana before the trick. Get a regular banana, unpeeled, and a clean straight pin. Pick a spot on the peel and stick the pin into it, as deep as you can without going through the other side. Then just wiggle the pin around, and you'll be slicing the banana inside the peel (see figure A). Do the same thing with the pin in four or five other spots, and you'll have a sliced banana inside the peel (see Figure B). The pinholes are so tiny that they're hard to see, and if you put them into dark spots on the banana, they'll be almost invisible.

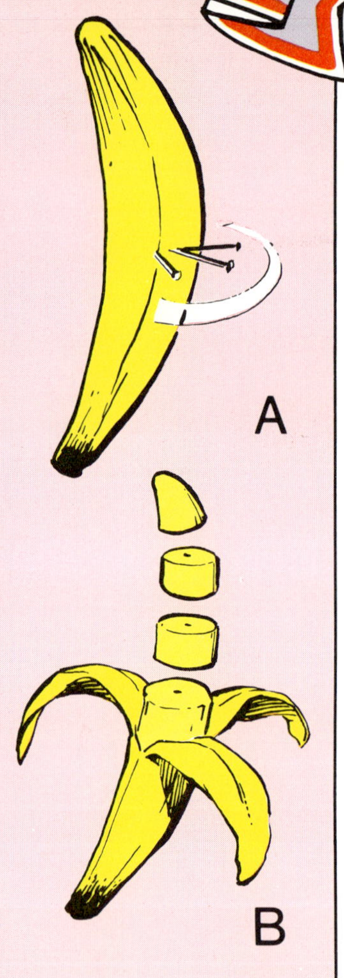

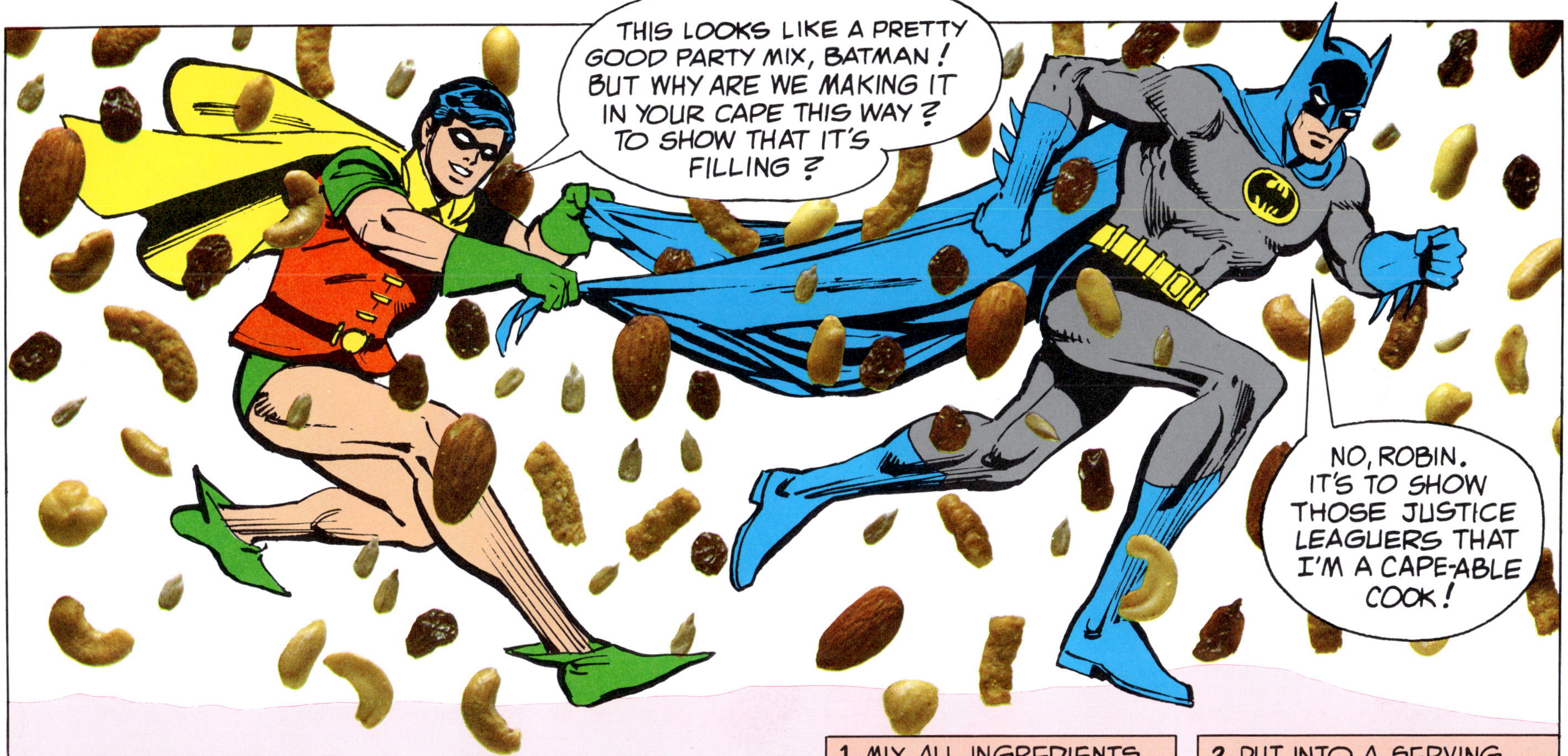

THIS LOOKS LIKE A PRETTY GOOD PARTY MIX, BATMAN! BUT WHY ARE WE MAKING IT IN YOUR CAPE THIS WAY? TO SHOW THAT IT'S FILLING?

NO, ROBIN. IT'S TO SHOW THOSE JUSTICE LEAGUERS THAT I'M A CAPE-ABLE COOK!

# BATMIX

**FOOD YOU NEED:**

½ Cup Nuts of Any Kind
½ Cup Raisins
½ Cup Sunflower Seeds
½ Cup Sesame Sticks

**TOOLS YOU NEED:**

Measuring Cup
Small Bowl
Mixing Spoon
Serving Dish

# SUPERMAN'S SUPER DELICIOUS

**FOOD YOU NEED:**

**For Brownie—**

1 Tablespoon Vegetable Oil
¾ Cup Brown Sugar
1 Cup Wheat Germ
¼ Cup Carob or Cocoa
½ Teaspoon Baking Powder
¼ Cup Vegetable Oil
2 Eggs
1 Teaspoon Vanilla

**For Ice Cream—**

½ Gallon Ice Cream or Frozen Yogurt—Any Flavor!

**For Frosting—**

½–¾ Cup Heavy Cream
1 Tablespoon Sugar (Brown, White) or Honey

**For Decorating—**

Any of These:
Strawberries, Raisins, Nuts, Chocolate or Carob Candy

**TOOLS YOU NEED:**

Measuring Spoons
Measuring Cup
Paper Towel or Napkin
Mixing Bowl
Mixing Spoon
Spring Form Pan or Tube Pan
Large Spoon
Butter Knife or Rubber Spatula
Plastic Wrap or Foil
Electric Mixer

**1.** PUT 1TBS. OIL IN SPRING-FORM PAN. SPREAD ON BOTTOM AND SIDES OF PAN WITH PAPER TOWEL.

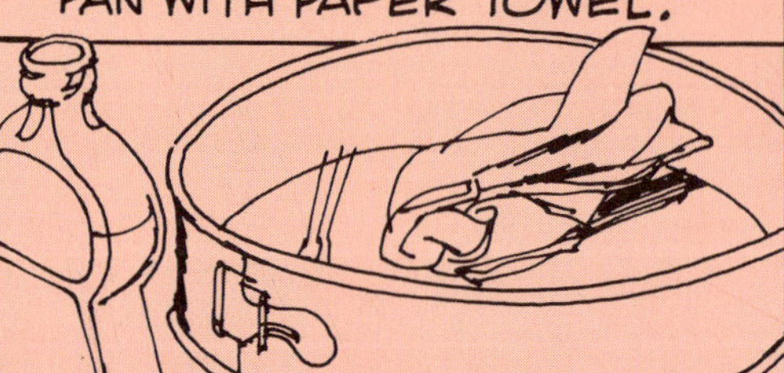

**2.** PUT ALL THE OTHER BROWNIE INGREDIENTS INTO BOWL.

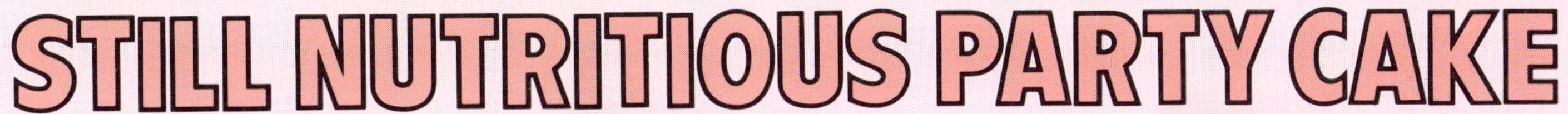


...WITH HEAT VISION I CAN BAKE IT...

...COOL IT WITH MY SUPER-COLD BREATH...

...AND NOW FLY IT TO THE PARTY. THIS SHOULD BE BIG ENOUGH, UNLESS ***GREEN ARROW*** STARTS SHOWING OFF HOW MUCH HE CAN PACK AWAY!

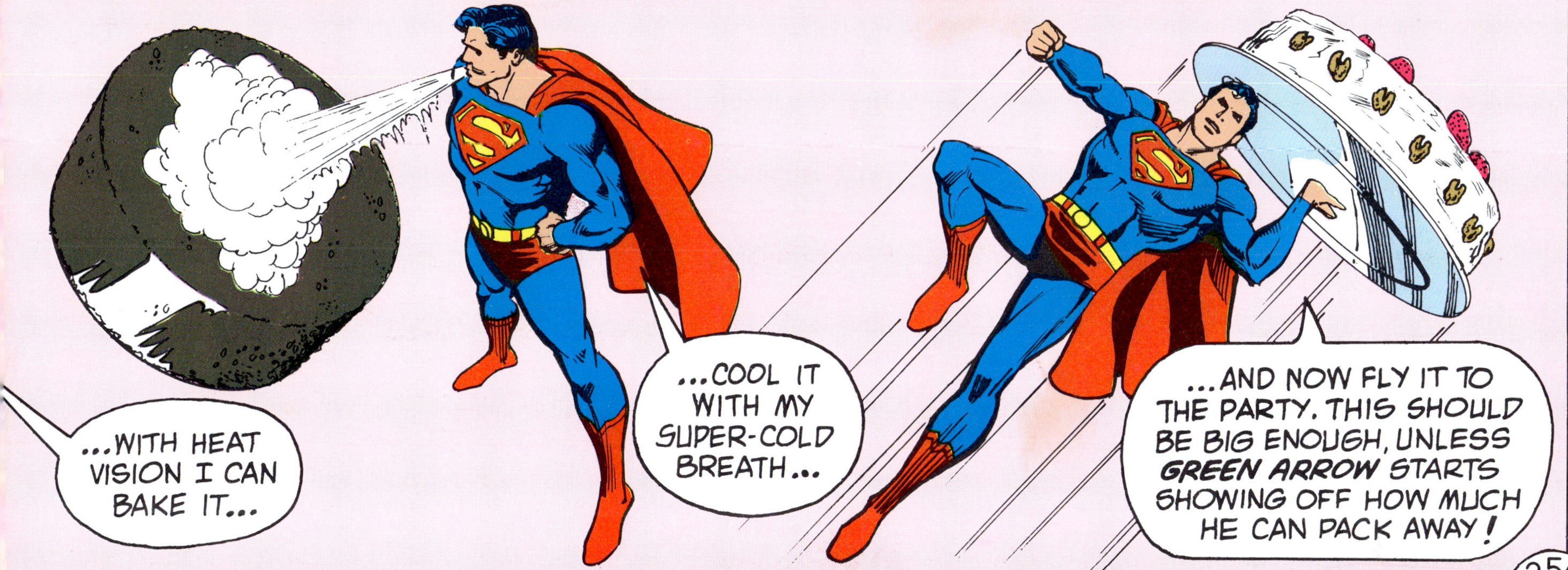

3. MIX WELL WITH MIXING SPOON. BATTER SHOULD BE THICK.

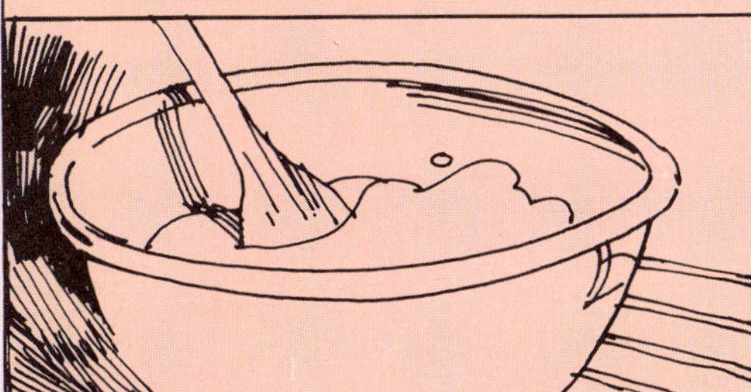

4. POUR BATTER INTO GREASED PAN. WITH SPOON, SPREAD EVENLY AROUND BOTTOM OF PAN.

5. PUT IN OVEN AND BAKE AT 350° FOR 20 MINUTES. LET THE BROWNIE COOL COMPLETELY BEFORE STARTING THE NEXT PART.

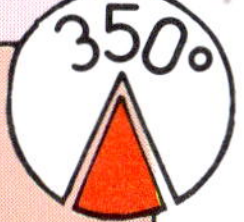

350°

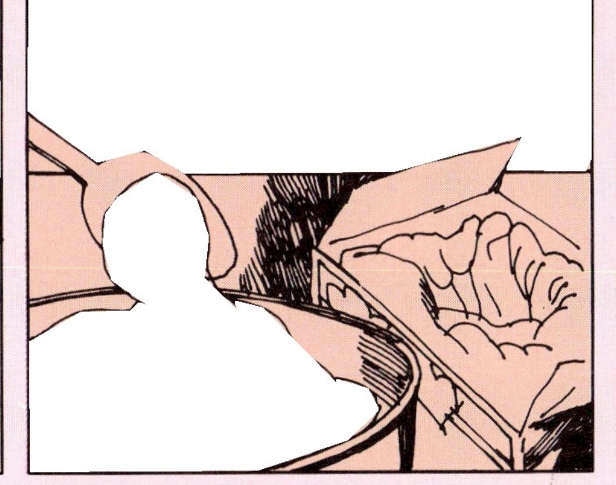

8. SPREAD ICE CREAM EVENLY USING BUTTER KNIFE OR RUBBER SPATULA.

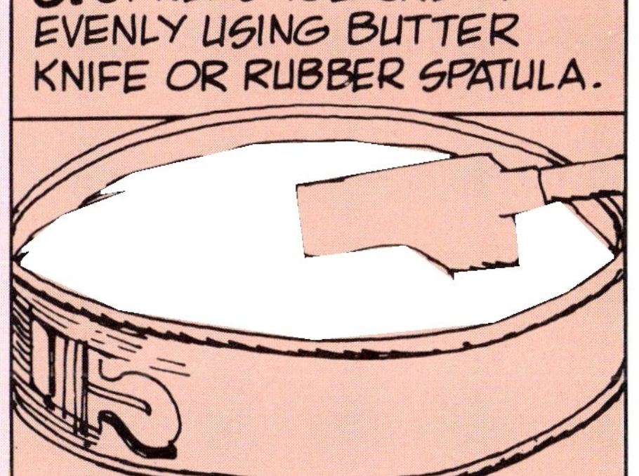

9. COVER PAN WITH FOIL OR PLASTIC WRAP. PUT IN FREEZER AT LEAST 5 HOURS OR OVERNIGHT.

10. TO MAKE FROSTING: PUT HEAVY CREAM AND SUGAR INTO MIXING BOWL.

11. BEAT WITH ELECTRIC MIXER UNTIL CREAM IS THICK AND STIFF AND LOOKS LIKE WHIPPED CREAM (*WHICH IT IS*).

TAKE THE ICE CREAM BROWNIE CAKE OUT OF FREEZER.

13. TO LOOSEN CAKE FROM PAN: WARM BUTTER KNIFE UNDER HOT WATER. CUT BETWEEN PAN AND CAKE.

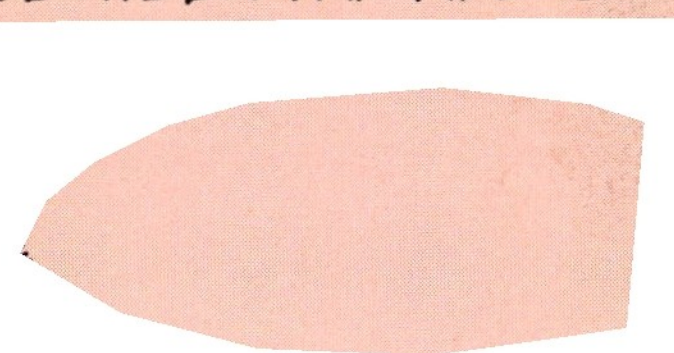

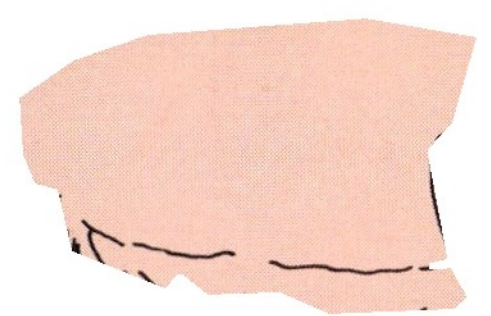

15. SPOON WHIPPED CREAM ONTO CAKE. SPREAD EVENLY ALL OVER TOP AND SIDES OF CAKE USING A BUTTER KNIFE OR RUBBER SPATULA. WORK QUICKLY SO ICE CREAM WON'T MELT.

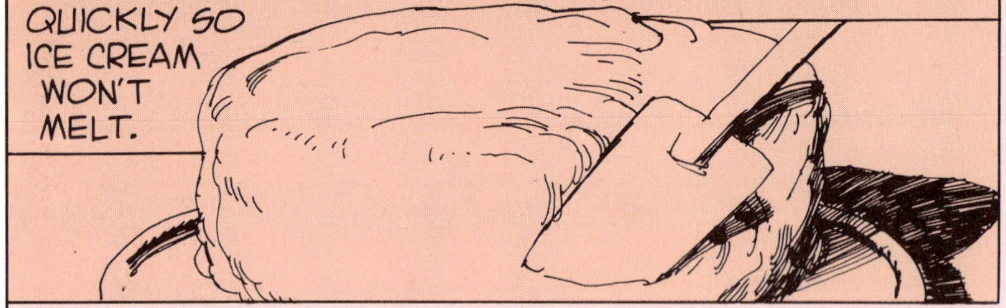

16. RETURN CAKE TO FREEZER. AFTER 2 HOURS CAKE CAN BE LOOSELY COVERED WITH FOIL OR PLASTIC WRAP.

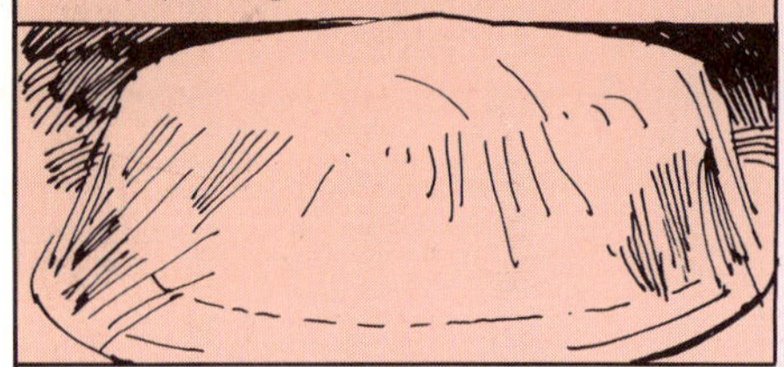

17. TAKE CAKE OUT OF FREEZER 5-10 MINUTES BEFORE SERVING SO THAT IT CAN SOFTEN. YOU CAN NOW DECORATE IT.

18. TO DECORATE:

USE STRAWBERRIES, RAISINS OR NUTS. YOU CAN SPELL A MESSAGE WITH THEM OR YOU CAN MAKE LETTERS BY MELTING 2 OR 3 OUNCES OF CHOCOLATE OR CAROB CANDY IN A PAN ON A VERY LOW FLAME.

WITH A SPOON, DROP CHOCOLATE ON WAX PAPER TO SPELL ANYTHING YOU WANT. A CLEAN WATER COLOR BRUSH WORKS WELL TOO. PUT WAX PAPER INTO FREEZER UNTIL CANDY HARDENS. THEN PUT ON CAKE.

6. TAKE ICE CREAM OUT OF FREEZER. WAIT AT LEAST 30-45 MINUTES FOR IT TO SOFTEN.

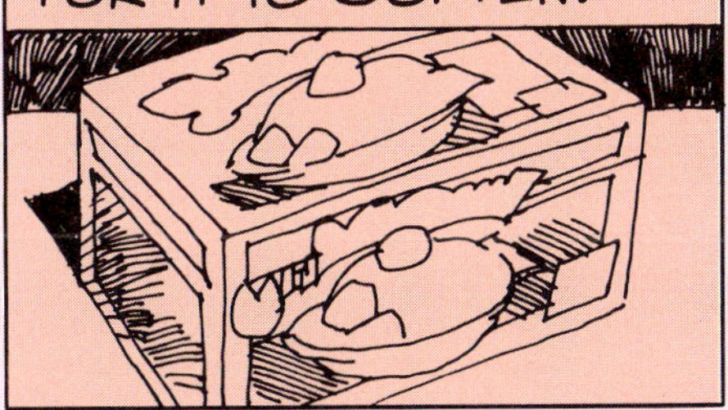

7. THEN SPOON SOFTENED ICE CREAM ON TO BROWNIE IN PAN. USE UP ALL THE ICE CREAM.

8. SPREAD ICE CREAM EVENLY USING BUTTER KNIFE OR RUBBER SPATULA.

9. COVER PAN WITH FOIL OR PLASTIC WRAP. PUT IN FREEZER AT LEAST 5 HOURS OR OVERNIGHT.

10. TO MAKE FROSTING: PUT HEAVY CREAM AND SUGAR INTO MIXING BOWL.

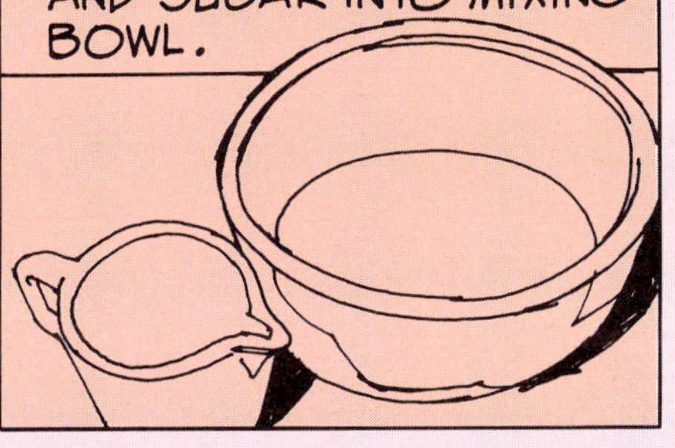

11. BEAT WITH ELECTRIC MIXER UNTIL CREAM IS THICK AND STIFF AND LOOKS LIKE WHIPPED CREAM (*WHICH IT IS*).

12. TAKE THE ICE CREAM BROWNIE CAKE OUT OF FREEZER.

13. TO LOOSEN CAKE FROM PAN: WARM BUTTER KNIFE UNDER HOT WATER. CUT BETWEEN PAN AND CAKE.

14. REMOVE SPRING-FORM PAN. BE VERY CAREFUL.

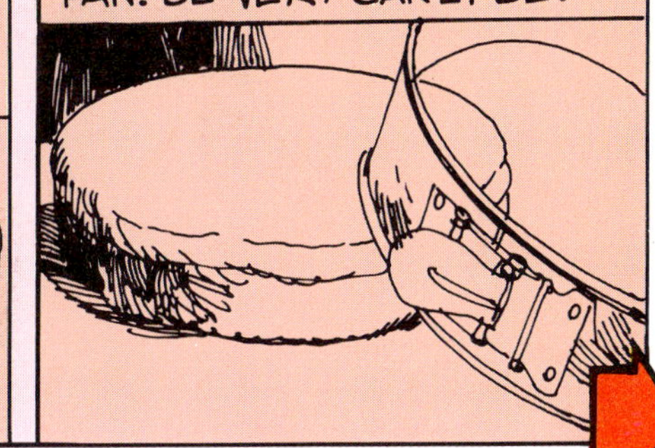

15. SPOON WHIPPED CREAM ONTO CAKE. SPREAD EVENLY ALL OVER TOP AND SIDES OF CAKE USING A BUTTER KNIFE OR RUBBER SPATULA. WORK QUICKLY SO ICE CREAM WON'T MELT.

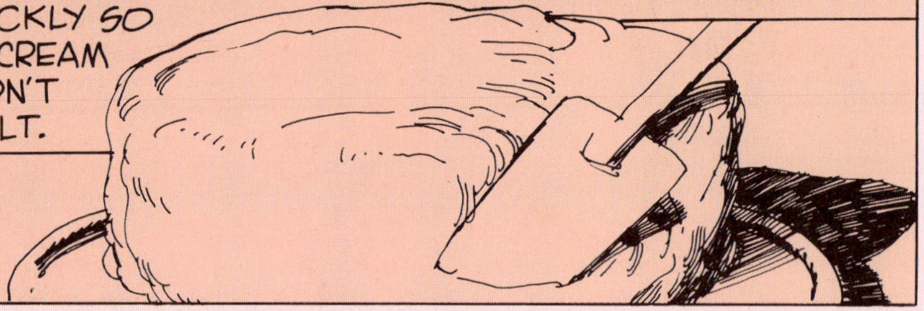

16. RETURN CAKE TO FREEZER. AFTER 2 HOURS CAKE CAN BE LOOSELY COVERED WITH FOIL OR PLASTIC WRAP.

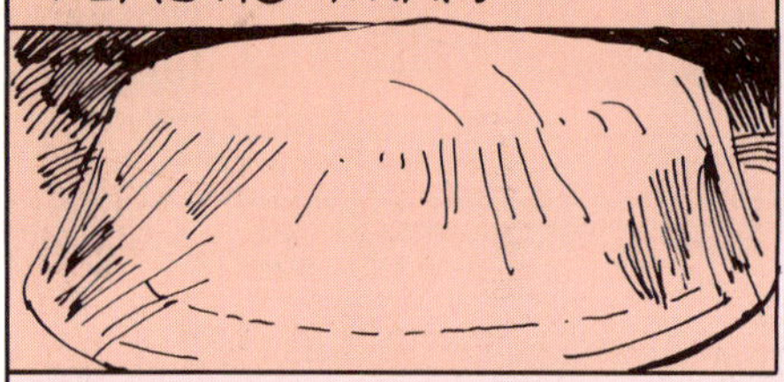

17. TAKE CAKE OUT OF FREEZER 5-10 MINUTES BEFORE SERVING SO THAT IT CAN SOFTEN. YOU CAN NOW DECORATE IT.

18. TO DECORATE:

USE STRAWBERRIES, RAISINS OR NUTS. YOU CAN SPELL A MESSAGE WITH THEM OR YOU CAN MAKE LETTERS BY MELTING 2 OR 3 OUNCES OF CHOCOLATE OR CAROB CANDY IN A PAN ON A VERY LOW FLAME.

WITH A SPOON, DROP CHOCOLATE ON WAX PAPER TO SPELL ANYTHING YOU WANT. A CLEAN WATER COLOR BRUSH WORKS WELL TOO. PUT WAX PAPER INTO FREEZER UNTIL CANDY HARDENS. THEN PUT ON CAKE.

HAPPY BIRTHDAY
JLA

# INDEX

FRYING PAN
PEELER
STRAINER (SIEVE)
MEASURING SPOONS
BLENDER
MEASURING CUP
ICE CREAM SCOOP
COLANDER
SPATULAS
RUBBER
REGULAR